Bar Style

This publication is designed to provide accurate and authoritative informa-
tion in regard to the subject matter covered. It is sold on the understanding
that the Publisher is not engaged in rendering professional services. If
professional advice or other expert assistance is required, the services of
a competent professional should be sought.

Other Wiley Editorial Offices

John Wiley & Sons Inc., 111 River Street, Hoboken, NJ 07030, USA

Jossey-Bass, 989 Market Street, San Francisco, CA 94103-1741, USA

Wiley-VCH Verlag GmbH, Boschstr. 12, D-69469 Weinheim, Germany

John Wiley & Sons Australia Ltd, 33 Park Road, Milton, Queensland 4064,
Australia

John Wiley & Sons (Asia) Pte Ltd, 2 Clementi Loop #02-01, Jin Xing
Distripark, Singapore 129809

John Wiley & Sons Canada Ltd, 22 Worcester Road, Etobicoke, Ontario,
Canada M9W 1L1

ISBN 0 470 11475 4

Printed and bound by Conti Tipocolor, Italy

Bar Style

Howard Watson

Series Designer Liz Sephton

contents

Executive Commissioning Editor: Helen Castle
Design and Editorial Management: Mariangela Palazzi-Williams
Editorial Assistance: Famida Rasheed

Acknowledgements

This book has been such a collaborative effort that there are far too many people to thank beyond the very tip of the iceberg, so I apologise to the dozens of unmentioned people who have given their invaluable time, resources and knowledge to help this endeavour. Architects, designers, hoteliers, club owners, publicists, photographers and their teams have all gone beyond the call of duty. The few people I can mention include Helen Castle, Mariangela Palazzi-Williams and Famida Rasheed of Wiley-Academy whose daily work would require of others alchemy and miracles. The book is greatly indebted to the visionary designer of the Interior Angles series, Liz Sephton, the intuitive and professional Lewis Derrick, and Tessa Clark. Particular thanks must go to Richard Scott, Mat Riches, Steve Gorton, Ollie Vigors and, as ever, Miranda Harrison.

Picture credits

Key: t=top, b=below, c=centre, l=left, r=right

Cover: Photo by Nicholas d'Archimbaud courtesy of Conran and Partners; pp 1, 113-17 Hotel Q!/Dirk Schaper; pp2-3, 68-9 Courtesy of Mirvac Hotels; pp 4(l), 108(t) Morley Von Sternberg/Arcaid; pp 4-5, 14, 16-17, 29-33, 48-51, 107, 108(b), 109, 110-11, 170-1, 174-7, 204-7 Morgans Hotel Group courtesy of Purple PR; pp 7(t), 10, 92(tl + bl) Guildhall Library, Corporation of London; pp 7(b), 178-81 Courtesy of The Ritz London; pp 8-9, 99-101, 221(m) Courtesy of The Savoy; pp 11-12, 19, 21-7 Photographs by Steve Gorton 07973 799110; pp 13, 35-7, 60-3, 102-3, 162-9 Courtesy of design hotels™ www.designhotels.com; pp 15, 143(bl) Courtesy of PROOF Consultancy Ltd; pp 39-43, 133, 173, 186-9, 217(tr + br) Courtesy of www.leonardo.com; pp 44-7 Courtesy of Douglas Wallace; pp 52-5 Courtesy of The Prince Hotel; pp 56-9 Courtesy of Campbell Gray Hotels; pp 65, 66(b), 67(b) Courtesy of Conran and Partners; pp 66(t), 67(t) Richard Learoyd; pp 70-1, 78-81 Photo by Nicholas d'Archimbaud courtesy of Conran and Partners; pp 73, 87-8, 89(t), 216(br) © Chris Gascoigne; pp 75-7 Courtesy of The Blue Bar, The Berkeley; pp 82-5, 222(r) Courtesy of Raffles; p 89(b) Plans courtesy of MoreySmith Limited; pp 91, 92(tr + br), 93 Photos © Martin Charles; pp 95-7 Courtesy of Claridge's; pp 105, 145-9, 214(tr) Photos by Koji Okamura courtesy of Conran and Partners; pp 119-23, 214(tl), 216(bl) Photos by Alberto Ferrero/AFS; pp 124-9, 213(b) Courtesy of Sketch; pp 130-2 Courtesy of Raffles The Plaza, Singapore; pp 134-7, 220(r) Courtesy of 60 Thompson; pp 139-42, 143(t + br), 224(l) Courtesy of City Inn; pp 151-3 Courtesy of The Fullerton, Singapore; pp 154-7 Courtesy of Ha_talská a.s. – Hotel Josef; pp 158-61 Courtesy of Merivale Group; pp 182-5 Rafael Viñoly Architects and Michael Kleinberg Photography; pp 191-3, 215(br), 216(tr), 217(bl) Courtesy of Plaza Athénée; pp 195-9, 212(r) Photos by Rafael Vargas Fotografía, SL; pp 201, 202(t), 203(t) Lonsdale courtesy of Brower Lewis Pelham PR; pp 202(b), 203(b) Courtesy of Lonsdale; pp 210-11, 215(t) Courtesy of Knoll, Inc; p 212(l) Courtesy of Fritz Hansen; p 213(tl) Courtesy of George Smith; pp 213(tr), 215(m) Courtesy of www.panik-design.com; p 214(bl + br) Courtesy of Conran Contracts; p 215(bl) Courtesy of O'Driscoll Furniture; p 216(tl) Courtesy of Alma; p 217(tl) Courtesy of McInnes Cook; pp 218-19, 220 (l + m), 221(l + r), 222(l), 223, 224(m + r) Courtesy of The Bombay Sapphire Image Library.

Brooks's, London. In JLR's 1810 depiction, a man stands outside the door of Brooks's, one of the gentlemen's clubs in Regency London

Dressed in a combination of Marc Jacobs couture, charity shop chic and a touch of the high street, they breeze confidently past the doorman and into the bar, their Manolos clacking lightly on the fossilised limestone. At the long, onyx blade of the counter, passionfruit martinis are ordered with barely a glance at the menu. They glance casually around the room at the familiar and famous people sitting on the pony-skin banquettes and oversized armchairs, allowing themselves slight, conspiratorial smiles. There is nowhere better to see and be seen …

They are among the new breed of drinker that has helped to create a monumental shift in bar culture and design since the mid-1990s, and their chosen destinations are hotel bars and private members' clubs. Pub chains and identikit bars have been forsaken in a search for quality, style and service in more exclusive, beautifully designed environments. This new breed should not be mistaken for the established, 'old money' elite. At its core are middle-income, 20- to 40-somethings with interests in fashion, design and media who wish to find an inspiring preserve away from the ever-increasing homogeneity of the high street. Previously dominated by sexless corporate design and traditional stuffiness, hotel and members' bars have led the revolution with interiors of great beauty, style and wit. The two genres have now started to merge in offering exclusive luxury, with more and more hotels having private members' bars.

The media has a frenzied love of these cool, fashionable bars, but the designs often rise above the *Zeitgeist*, offering a quality of aesthetic experience that should endure longer than the celebrity of some of the customers.

Introduction

Hotels and cocktails – an ongoing love affair

Naturally, refreshments and lodging have always been linked. Hotel culture in Britain came out of the medieval precedent of inns that provided food, drink, shelter and stabling for the weary, and relatively rare, traveller. The United States, with its population of migrants and its frontier history, has always had a very strong lodgings culture. In the 17th century, many towns in the eastern and middle territories had an 'ordinary' for board and liquor. Through these precursors

The Ritz, London. Elevation of the Ritz. The 1906 facade has remained virtually untouched

to the tavern, the Puritan establishment hoped to regulate the sale of alcohol – a visitor would sometimes find his desire for full inebriation hampered by an unwelcome guest who was there solely to monitor his consumption. In the towns ordinaries gave way to taverns while, out West, there was a later proliferation of almost temporary, wooden hotels that often housed saloon bars.

Worldwide, the idea of luxury hotels related to travel as a pleasurable exercise didn't really burgeon until late Victorian and Edwardian times, which saw the establishment of the Savoy and the Ritz in London, although there are early exceptions such as Isaiah Rogers's Tremont Hotel, which already had plumbing when it was opened in Boston in 1826. Once such hotels had been established, however, they were always associated with the consumption of expensive alcohol in rarefied public spaces. Right from the outset, they offered what can be termed a 'social space', attracting local socialites as well as hotel guests to their bars, and they have a long association with cocktails. There are countless theories as to the origin of the word 'cocktail', which variously include birds' plumage, French egg-cups, horses' tails and a Mexican princess called Coctel. The term's first recorded use was in America in 1806, but it remains difficult to ascertain the historical link between a dry martini and the docked tail of a horse.

Often referred to as 'American drinks', modern cocktails really made their mark in Britain with the opening of the bar at Claridge's in 1899, displacing the more European convention of the aperitif. According to the *Sphere* newspaper at that time, barmaid Ada Coleman, who was appointed at the suggestion of Richard D'Oyly Carte, was the first woman to mix and serve cocktails in Britain, starting off with a Manhattan. D'Oyly Carte had established the Savoy Hotel in 1889, primarily to provide an overnight service for the patrons who came to his productions of Gilbert and Sullivan operettas at the theatre next door. Coleman

The Savoy, London. Seen here in 1931, the American Bar at the Savoy was a leading light of the golden age of the cocktail and sported an adventurous Art Deco design

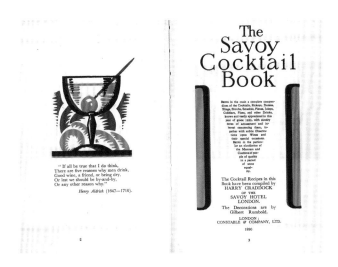

The Savoy, London. *The Savoy Cocktail Book*, compiled by Harry Craddock in 1930, remains in print

moved to the Savoy's American Bar in 1903, where she continued to serve cocktails until 1924, reportedly bowing out with a martini for the Prince of Wales. The American Bar is the oldest extant cocktail bar in London. Bars with the same name survive at the Connaught and Stafford, also in London, and the Hotel de Paris in Monte Carlo as testaments to the birth of the modern cocktail.

Cocktails were extremely popular in the United States during the Prohibition era as they disguised the taste of bootlegged and home-made alcohol. Effectively, during the 1920s they progressed from the dive of the speakeasy to the most refined hotels of Europe. Barman Harry Craddock made that journey too, and was appointed head bartender at the Savoy in 1925. He became a legend, devising many cocktails and compiling *The Savoy Cocktail Book*, which remains in print to this day as part of the hotel's *Cocktails – The Present from the Past*. Bars in many of the leading luxury hotels were given sumptuous Art Deco (or Art Moderne as it was known) makeovers and it is the style of their late 1920s and 1930s interiors that provides the enduring image of cocktail sophistication. These years turned out to be the golden age for both cocktails and hotel bars, and some of the latest contemporary interiors still make reference to that era. Cocktails continued to remain popular with the upper classes until the late 1950s, when the hotel drinking culture came to be seen as old-fashioned, and more casual nightclubs and music venues emerged.

Unfortunately, post-war hotel architecture can be characterised by poor, unimaginative shells housing identical units and corporate spaces. Defying the earlier history of hotels, many of the new builds lacked interesting social spaces. Later, bars and restaurants were created with conferences and the corporate market in mind, and housed mundane, stifling and badly thought-through interior design. For the most part, a modern inner-city hotel was the last place anyone would go if they were in search of either entertainment or style.

When the cocktail culture re-emerged significantly in the 1980s it typified the brashness of the gaudy, 'me generation' of flash yuppies, and was less expressly associated with hotels. Fortunately, the pink neon of this era's bars has all but flickered its last and the cocktail has returned to the refined environment of the hotel bar. The new wave of designs is the perfect recipient for the renewal of interest in this distinct type of social space, while some of the original hotel bars have gained a level of cultural prestige, or kudos, that was beyond them even in the 1920s. The new cocktail cognoscenti have a sophisticated awareness of taste and style, which should indicate that this interest, and the consequent stretching of design boundaries, is here to stay.

From gentlemen's clubs to private bars

In terms of social spaces in the early 20th century, the hotel bar's principal contender for the loyalty of the privileged was the gentlemen's club. Bizarrely British (and subsequently British colonial) institutions, the clubs grew out of the 17th- and 18th-century coffee and chocolate houses where the aristocracy met informally for the purposes of conversation, politics and, primarily, gambling. These became private clubs largely because aristocrats were wary of being fleeced by untrustworthy commoners rather than by each other. The Cocoa-Tree House included Byron among its members and, in the 17th century, was the base for the Jacobites, the supporters of the exiled Stuart dynasty. During the Regency period, membership of gentlemen's clubs such as the still extant White's (a former chocolate house founded in 1693), Boodle's and Brooks's, a favourite with the dandyish Whigs, was *de rigueur* for aristocrats. Men of means were usually members of at least one club. It was within the walls of these

establishments that fortunes were won and lost, outrageous entertainment was had and business was done. The décor was usually indicative of the tastes of the era's private houses, with comfortable seating, marble fire-surrounds and a mass of fine upholstery.

Later in the 19th century club culture became more conservative, with less emphasis on gambling, and both the architecture and interior design established our current perception of the gentlemen's club. There was a tremendous wave of new establishments, brought about by the emergence of the new professional, middle classes. Clubs often consisted of grand but very masculine rooms, including a library, dining room, lounge, and smoking and gaming rooms, in solid, neoclassical buildings. Their political nature persisted, with the Reform Club set up by liberal supporters of the extension of the franchise, first granted by the Reform Act of 1832, while the Carlton Club continues to have close associations with the Conservative Party. Other clubs had their basis in cultural or occupational allegiances such as travelling (the Travellers' Club, designed by Sir Charles Barry, could be joined only by those who had been further than 500 miles from London) or science, literature and art (the Athenaeum, designed by Decimus Burton).

The architecture of the clubs rarely gave more than a hint of their associations. At a casual glance you could easily be forgiven for confusing the United Services, Athenaeum, Travellers' and Reform clubs that form a lengthy tribute to classicism along Pall Mall. On closer inspection it becomes apparent that, suitably, it is the Athenaeum that has Doric columns supporting a portico topped off with a statue of Pallas Athena, but the exterior of the Travellers' Club gives no suggestion that the architect himself ever travelled much further than next door. The Reform Club is designed around a central courtyard in the manner of an Italian palazzo, but any attempt to equate the symmetry of the four sides with an evocation of democracy is a thankless task.

There has always been a very strong element of intrigue and social exclusion in private clubs and these broad, plain facades help, perhaps deliberately, to reinforce their communal mask. It is really the interiors – the portraits on the walls, the origins of objects, the size and contents of the library – that hint at major distinctions of purpose. As yet, few older clubs have made an architectural transition towards transparency but the recent redesign of the

The Reform Club, London. Established out of political sympathies, the Reform Club was completed in 1842, and joined a stretch of Victorian clubs along Pall Mall. It was designed by Sir Charles Barry, who went on to be the principal architect of the Houses of Parliament

1868 Commonwealth Club provides a good example of how this can be done. However, even today's new clubs often choose to have discreet entrances that lead to an Aladdin's cave in which their true purpose is revealed.

Many of the traditional clubs are still going today, and both their décor and rules of membership are often remarkably unchanged. Membership can only be proposed from within and must then be endorsed by a committee; and many still refuse full membership to women. The days when Sheridan's application for membership of Brooks's was rebuffed three times on the grounds that his father had appeared on the stage may have gone, but Lady Thatcher remains the only full female member of the Carlton, having been given honorary status. Even the Athenaeum, which could be presumed to be progressive because of its close association with the arts, allowed full membership to women only in 2002.

The model of the gentlemen's club in Britain was copied overseas, particularly in parts of the empire like Australia and India. Some still survive – as they do in the United States, although most clubs there are based on academic or sporting ties.

In Britain the wave of significant new gentlemen's clubs effectively died out in the 1920s. A different type of private members' club had already begun to emerge, harking back to the original, heady days of 17th- and 18th-century hedonism rather than Victorian, strait-laced conformity. The Chelsea Arts Club, primarily made up of artists and writers, had been founded in 1891 at the suggestion of Whistler. It was, and remains, consciously bohemian: in some ways it is the precursor of modern members' clubs with their predilection for both the arts and excess. Several other clubs help to form a somewhat addled, hazy chain of connections into the modern era. The Colony Room Club was founded in 1948, and still stands as the antithesis to the traditional club. Its interior is an eclectic ramble through post-war art. 1962 saw the new wave of comedians and satirists of the time, led by Peter Cook, opening their own take on club culture by converting a former strip-joint in Soho. Ironically called the Establishment, its club status meant that performers could avoid the censorship that was plaguing British performance at the time, and members could revel in irreverence often directed at real establishment figures sitting in the smoking rooms of their own clubs less than a mile away. It was more than just a comedy venue, with the basement Jazz Bar, which often featured Dudley Moore tinkling the ivories, taking on a life of its own. The Establishment was short-lived, but it helped to pave the way for a surprising marriage between club culture and nonconformity.

Other links with the new type of club that took off in the mid-1990s included the Zanzibar. While the Colony Room and the Establishment eschewed architecturally designed interiors the Zanzibar, which opened in 1976, was a very consciously designed space full of features, such as the curved zigzag of the bar, that emphasised social possibilities. It is no surprise that one of the designers, Tchaik Chassay, went on to design the Groucho.

The Groucho Club, London. The Groucho was set up on Dean Street in 1985, when Soho was still a run-down area brimming with highly visible sex shops

New wave

Until the mid-1990s, it was unimaginable that hotel and private members' bars would be the choice of social venue for so many urbanites. However, Britain was in the grip of Cool Britannia, while on television 'Sex and the City' was defining a new obsession with style. Founded in 1985, the Groucho was popular with the publishing world from the start, but its full impact wasn't really appreciated until nearly a decade later when it became a media sensation. It broke away from the usual concept of a club and was a hotbed for the youthful artists and musicians who seemed to hold the world in the palms of their hands. Soon afterwards, in

1997, the Met Bar at London's Metropolitan Hotel became a tabloid dream, feeding a media lust for celebrity that seems to grow with no prospect of diminishing.

Meanwhile, in the United States, Ian Schrager had revolutionised the concept of the modern hotel with the 'boutique hotel', a phrase he says he fashioned with his now-deceased partner Steve Rubell. The two men had run the infamous New York nightclub Studio 54, so they knew more than a little about capturing the mood of the times before they moved into the hotel market. The facilities in their hotels attracted a great deal of attention, and not just from guests. The Skybar at the Mondrian in Los Angeles led the way in 1996, and over the years Philippe Starck's designs for Schrager became increasingly unique and ironic, playing a pivotal role in the democratisation of the hotel – the redefining of the social space. The Light Bar at the St Martin's Lane in London was initially shocking, forcing critics and customers alike to reconsider what they expected of a hotel bar; but Starck went further with the Hudson Bar at the Hudson in New York, and with both the Purple Bar and the Long Bar at the Sanderson in London. In recent years David Collins has excelled at reinventing the public spaces of previously traditional hotels that have caught the mood (or understood the financial benefits) for dynamically designed bars. Established designers such as Terence Conran, David Chipperfield and fashion designer John Rocha have placed a new emphasis on hotels and their public areas. Suddenly hotels are at the forefront of contemporary design and their bars are their showrooms.

Beyond the Groucho, the new breed of members' bars is growing incredibly fast, and this is not confined to London. Both New York and London have a Soho House and a Milk and Honey. The latter, which decries any media interest, has unique house rules that are a perverse echo of those of traditional clubs, and a

The Groucho Club, London. The main bar at the club combines luxury and comfort, and has remained largely unchanged over the last 20 years. The Soho Bar upstairs was overhauled in 2004, giving members a more contemporary, but still understated, alternative meeting place

wicked response to the cult of celebrity that helped to foster the fortunes of the new ones. They begin with the words 'No name-dropping, no star f**king', and continue with 'Gentlemen will not introduce themselves to ladies. Ladies, feel free to start a conversation or ask the bartender to introduce you.' An important aspect of the reinvention of hotel and members' bars is that they appeal to women.

Sex and the City

The television series is dead and buried, but the reference lives on. 'Sex and the City' is a cheap and overused handle, but it nevertheless captures something that is germane to this new culture.

Whatever the quality of their design, ultracool hotel and members' bars wouldn't have happened if there wasn't an eager clientele waiting for them. It can't be denied that a certain amount of stargazing follows media exposure of the

The Metropolitan, London. When the Met Bar opened in 1997 it set a new trend for private member's bars within hotels

The Hudson, New York. As a result of Philippe Starck's design, the Hudson Bar at Ian Schrager's 2000 hotel soon became one of New York's most celebrity-heavy bars

drinking hole of a film or pop star, but the popularity of these places goes beyond an obsession with celebrity. It is about a cultural psyche that has been born out of a combination of economic, environmental, social and aesthetic factors. Fleeing from the ubiquitous uberpub chains and bars-by-numbers that dominate the high streets of Britain, style-conscious urbanites make for hotel and members' bars that increasingly deliver bespoke, exquisite and crafted surroundings. We are in a duplicitous age of individualism and anonymity. The desire of the individual to break free, and the propensity to self-reward along the lines of the 'Sex and the City' characters, have never been higher, while the urban landscape is becoming more and more homogenised. That hotel bars and members' clubs are safe, protected environments has been significant in establishing a female-biased customer profile.

Drinking tastes have also become more sophisticated as part of a wider social change. Because people are having children at a later age, there is an older, wiser, cash-rich and fashion-savvy clientele that has had its fill of beer and the Saturday-night melee. They prefer to sip a caipirinha in refined, custom-designed surroundings. Hotel bars and members' clubs – which have extraordinarily similar customers in that, increasingly, there are members' bars within hotels – provide cultural oases.

Democracy and diversification

There is a trick that both hotel bars and members' clubs have to pull off. In order to balance a concept of 'cool' with a primary fiscal need, they have to be both exclusive and democratic. They must appeal to a wide clientele in the first place, but also make anyone who passes through their doors feel that they are among the select few.

The clubs are naturally exclusive, but if they seem to be too grand, overconcerned with their status or undemocratic in the way they treat their members, they will lose members or fail to attract new ones. Unlike a club such as White's, they cannot rely on upper-class loyalty and have to appeal across the classes. Celebrities are attracted to the privacy and exclusiveness they offer, but the criterion of membership is often simply the ability to pay the annual fee.

Modern hotel – and hotel bar – design is greatly aware of the social environment. It leans towards a new-found translucency that encourages nonresidents through the doors, in contrast to the tradition of braided livery, and revolving doors leading into an unseen environment, which create a physical and cultural barrier that stops anyone other than guests breaching the facade. Some hotel bars have their own entrances, while others rely on a lavish use of glass to entice people into a stylish lobby and onwards to the bar. Starck, for example, has made sure that the visual journey to the Light Bar at the St Martin's Lane starts in the street outside the main doors, while the joys of the Long Bar are hinted at through almost sheer curtains along the Sanderson's glass facade.

Architect-designed hotels have become firmly established as an international phenomenon: change has come, and it has been rapid. Hotels are a leading sector of contemporary design culture, and no aspect of their design is more significant than their social space: the lobbies, the restaurants and, principally, the bars. These are the elements that help to establish a hotel's reputation and give it a cultural kudos beyond the realms of tourism. This is extremely welcome. The travel industry is in a sustained period of trouble, as a result of the 11 September 2001 attack on the World Trade Center, and the war in Iraq. To an extent quite unimaginable before the 1990s, bars and restaurants that are open to the public – the democratisation of hotel facilities – provide a major source of revenue. They are full of local city-dwellers, and a hotel's fashionability and financial stability are not completely dependent on the guests upstairs or corporate shindigs in 'the ballroom'. But the city-dwellers who are helping to sustain the hotels' fortunes are style-savvy media types who have their own agendas. The pivotal element that draws them into the bars is design, so the designs have to deliver. However, there is a need to be artful. A dark and mysterious Arabian cave may be the bar style of the season, but will it also work as the setting for guests' breakfasts or an afternoon business meeting?

The diversification of the hotel's relationship with its environment coincides with a broader trend for diversification in retail. Rem Koolhaas's Prada in SoHo, New York, doubles up as an auditorium while Nicole Farhi's fashion boutique leads down to her restaurant. Following the Barnes & Noble lead, major bookshops are almost expected to provide a café – Waterstone's on London's Piccadilly has gone one better and has a swish top-floor bar that overlooks the city's skyline. Restaurants have also evolved, and this has aided the rise of the members' club. Teatro was born with a members' bar, Momo has its own private one, and several other major new ventures will also offer a restaurant/members' bar combination.

It seems that good hotel-bar design is here to stay and that there is a growing market for members' clubs. This book is not a thorough catalogue of the best bars in the world, but it is representative of what has happened in interior design since the mid-1990s – from the new wave to the consequent reaction of established hotels, and on to the latest interiors. The bars have been chosen partly because they promise to be durable within a notoriously fickle market; but only time will tell.

City Inn Westminster, London. Interior designers are under more pressure than ever to create cool, unique bars in new hotels. PROOF Consultancy created a sexy but multifunctional lounge to suit the needs of the new City Inn

the new wave

The reinvigoration of the design of private members' clubs and hotel bars, and those bars that are a hybrid of both, may have gained momentum from the mid-1990s onwards, but its roots are found a decade earlier, with the opening of Morgans Hotel in New York and the Groucho Club in London. Morgans was the first 'boutique hotel' established by Ian Schrager and his late partner Steve Rubell. The phrase is now used so broadly as to be meaningless, but at the time this type of hotel was a new departure, offering guests a personal experience laced with great attention to style and beauty. The concept was bound up with 'lobby socialising' in an environment that was in sharp contrast to the airport-terminal-thoroughfare style that dominated corporate hotels. The bar was, of course, crucial to a new, socially interactive hotel. Designed by Andrée Putnam, Morgans may be more understated than the later Schrager/Philippe Starck creations, but it provided the template for the reinvention of the social space of hotels that came to fruition in late 1990s projects such as the St Martin's Lane in London.

Within a year of Morgans, the Groucho had opened in London. While Schrager battled against the conformity of hotels, the Groucho took on the time-warped stuffiness of private members' clubs. It created a new exclusiveness for those who depended on their creative minds, rather than

The New Wave

bequests, for their fortunes. Membership was to become par for the course for a new, creative generation of young British artists, writers, actors and musicians who, by 1995, appeared to have the world at their feet. At the Groucho they could enjoy the protection and comforts of a club, while still holding two fingers up to the establishment. The Groucho's success led to Soho House, and to a still-growing roster of private members' bars. These include the Met Bar, for guests and private members, at the Metropolitan Hotel. When it opened in 1997, it was hard to imagine that it could survive in a hotel environment. The precedent it set is now being copied all over the world – with the proviso that if a bar isn't well designed, the clientele won't come in the first place.

The key to the success of exclusive hotel bars and members' clubs is luxury, but this is a concept that has been interpreted differently from the very beginnings of the new wave. A motif for Schrager and Philippe Starck is 'hotel as theatre'; a symbiotic relationship is forged between the physical space and the individuals who grace it. By contrast, members of the Groucho want a place where they can stop acting. In Schrager's terms, luxury is not a question of material wealth. It is found in a continual access to new experiences, so objects are humorously or ironically placed to disconcert or to surprise. At the Groucho, luxury is a familiar home from home, a protected, stylish but relaxed retreat.

Concepts of luxury may differ, but there are similarities in their execution. There is, of course, an emphasis on stylish design that unites all the projects in this book, but there are also more subtle connections. So much of 1900s and 1990s design appeared to be heading in the same direction that corporatism even inhabited the home: all the elements within a design matched, and the whole was similar to its neighbours. By contrast the Groucho, the Schrager hotels and many other spaces that helped to create the new wave were all about eclecticism, allowing rogue designs from different eras to rub shoulders and create an individual ambience. For their clientele they were oases that offered the real luxury of uniqueness in a desert of homogeneity and design conformity.

The Groucho Club, London. The Groucho, which celebrates its 20th anniversary in 2005, marked a new departure for private members' clubs. The main bar remains much as it was, revelling in eclectic 'shabby chic'

The Groucho Club

Melissa North-Chassay/David Bentheim

Location: London
Completion date: 1985–2004

Celebrating its 20th anniversary in 2005, the Groucho Club is the forefather of the modern private members' club. While newer clubs and hotel members' bars emerged with radical interiors – and rapid overhauls – to shake their tail feathers at the design-savvy, media cognoscenti, the main bar at the Groucho has remained virtually untouched since the first year of the club's inception. This has nothing to do with complacency or inertia: quite simply, the design works for the members. In other areas, where the owners feel they could offer more to the membership, design and function have progressed, culminating in the 2004 redesign of the upstairs Soho Bar.

The Groucho – its name was inspired by the Groucho Marx quote, 'I don't want to belong to any club that will accept me as a member' – may have been the forerunner of a new breed that acts as an antidote to the stuffiness of Victorian clubs, but its roots are surprisingly traditional. When the publishers Liz Calder and Carmen Callil first talked about their desire for a women-friendly club that would be a hub for literary London, their reference point was traditional gentlemen's clubs like the Garrick and the Reform. In fact, interior designer Melissa North-Chassay (who worked on the Groucho with her partner, the architect Tchaik Chassay) reveals that she consciously avoided the contemporary vogue for chrome and black, and that the real inspiration for the main bar came from the Algonquin in New York. The hotel, built in 1902, is famous for its association with Dorothy Parker and the Round Table. When North-Chassay went to see it, it was full of eclectic, shabby but cosy furniture. It felt convivial, unpretentious and homely. To this day, these words sum up the main bar at the Groucho. When the club opened the interior was more colourful than it is today, with apple-green covers adding brightness, but practicality and a warm snugness soon took hold. Dark leather chesterfields, red velvet armchairs, low lighting and art-strewn walls conspire to create exactly the right balance between luxury and comfort. The reason for the Groucho's continuing success is not that the media is obsessed with its members; rather, it is because its design (among other things) so endearingly entices the membership in the first place.

The club has a tan leather brasserie and, upstairs, a more formal restaurant. The latter, and the staircase up to it, are the architectural wonders that Tchaik Chassay brought to life during the building's conversion from a faded Trusthouse Forte property. The redesigned Soho Bar, consisting of three rooms, is also upstairs. The new, solid-looking bar counter is topped with grey granite and stands opposite an elegant, C-shaped, brown leather banquette. Much of the furniture is made up of red, rusty orange and deep lilac armchairs, while two of the rooms feature oval ceiling recesses that emit aureoles of light. The design is classy, stylish and contemporary without being too showy, and there are textural and chromatic links to the main bar.

Since the early 1990s the Groucho has had a strengthening relationship with artists, in addition to the writers and publishers who were the focus of its original membership. The Soho Bar, which used to act as an ad hoc function room, is a good space in which to show some of its collection of contemporary works, which are often infused with the same wit that gave rise to the club in the first place.

Opposite: **The Groucho Club, London.** Soho has become the bar and restaurant centre of London since the Groucho opened in 1985, when the area was a run-down warren for a very visible sex-industry. The emblem on the flag is the club's duck logo, inspired by the Marx Brothers film *Duck Soup*

Club	The Groucho Club
Address	45 Dean Street, London W1V 5AP, UK
Telephone	+44 (0)20 7439 4685
Opening hours	Mon–Sat 8.30am–2am
Number of seats	Main bar 40
Design style	Cosy, shabby-chic downstairs with a light, contemporary bar upstairs
Clientele	The upper echelons of the creative industries along with Soho bohemians
Speciality drinks/cocktails	Classic cocktails
Music	Piano music every night
Membership details/ door policy	Members only. Applications must be endorsed by two existing members

Below: **The Groucho Club, London.** The counter in the main bar curves around towards the front of the space. Part of the club's collection of art is displayed on the walls, which also feature a series of mirrors to create spaciousness. The red velvet chairs in the background recall the originally brighter coverings in the bar

Right: **The Groucho Club, London.** The main bar faces on to the street. The eclectic mix of furniture includes red and brown leather chesterfields and purple velvet sofas

Below, right: **The Groucho Club, London.** In the main bar the chesterfields are battered and comfortable

Above: The Groucho Club, London. David Bentheim's 2004 redesign of the three-room Soho Bar includes a granite-topped bar counter, and a silver and glass chandelier, created by Patrice Butler, in the centre of the ceiling recess

Left: The Groucho Club, London. The new counter in the Soho Bar has a black frontage, with a grey granite top and pediment which give it an authoritative but graceful weight. As in the main bar downstairs, mirrors are used to enhance the space

Above: **The Groucho Club, London.** Part of the club's art collection is displayed on the walls of the Soho Bar. The tables are decorated with the Groucho logo

Above: **The Groucho Club, London.** The third room in the Soho Bar has blood-orange walls, while the lighting in the ceiling recess creates a bright aureole

Above: **The Groucho Club, London.** The quieter, green room of the Soho Bar is five steps down from the main room. It has orange leather furniture, and two writing desks in case members have a sudden burst of creativity

Above: The Groucho Club, London. The formal
dining room sits under the grand arc of the ceiling
and the large skylight. Traditional dining chairs are
covered in mauve and a mulberry banquette runs
along the back wall

Opposite, above: **The Groucho Club, London.**
The brasserie reflected in the mirrors of an alcove

Opposite, below: **The Groucho Club, London.**
With brown panelling and a long leather banquette,
the brasserie is on the ground floor behind the bar,
and was also refurbished by David Bentheim

Skybar, Mondrian

Philippe Starck

Location: Los Angeles
Completion date: 1996

In design terms, the Skybar at the Mondrian is extraordinarily simple, but in social terms it set a new benchmark for the popularity of hotel bars as social gathering points for the rich and famous: it has become a cocktail lounger's legend. An Ian Schrager hotel, the Mondrian has a Sunset Boulevard address and combines a relaxed, outdoor, West Coast mentality with the glamour and fantasy that lie at the heart of Los Angeles' fame. With an emphasis on light, and with delicate furnishings, Philippe Starck's interiors include his typically careful placement of unusual and thought-provoking objects. However, the Skybar is little more than an open-air hut, supported by logs and capped by a tin roof. Wall-scaling ivy and flowering vines give it depth, while its armchairs and bar stools are inspired by American court and schoolhouse styles. Its coup is its unrivalled, panoramic views of Los Angeles. The Brad Pitts, etc., who first graced the Skybar found they could relax outdoors with like-minded celebrities while viewing the city they had conquered.

The design of the Skybar at the Mondrian is important because it led to another, more sophisticated Skybar development on the other side of America. One of Ian Schrager and Philippe Starck's skills has been to continue to adapt initial themes through later projects – the indoor/outdoor lobby at the Mondrian and at London's Sanderson originated at Schrager's Delano in Miami in 1995. The Skybar theme found its maturity in his Shore Club.

The Shore Club had opened in 2000 just a few blocks away from the Delano, which had been reigning supreme as South Beach's premium destination. As an Art Deco building revitalised by David Chipperfield, the Shore should have threatened the Delano's crown but never did. Schrager, though, saw the potential in his hotel's new neighbour and returned to Miami to take over its management in 2002. His most important intervention was to overhaul its leisure and outdoor facilities with, most importantly, a new Skybar. Starck was on hand again to realise his vision.

The bar has three principal areas, influenced by a sensual, Moroccan theme. The RedRoom is the main indoor space. Crimson lacquer is used to create a warm, sophisticated tone, covering the teak floor, the long, unbroken banquette and even the pool table. Handwoven, silk-covered pillows, flowing curtains and silver-covered, Napoleon III slipper-chairs add to the decadence. Outside, the colonnade in the RedRoom Garden is dressed with sheer, white curtains. Furnishings include a wrought-iron four-poster bed, teak stools, fibreglass chairs and a Nicaraguan hammock, lit by lanterns. The Skybar also includes the RumBar, with multicoloured concrete day beds and a lantern-lit pergola. Away from the hubbub, in the SandBar, guests relax on plantation-style chairs and feel the sand between their toes.

By 2002 the American music industry's fascination with the South Beach, sun-and-party lifestyle was faltering, but the exclusive, decadent Skybar has done much to reinvigorate it.

Opposite: Mondrian, Los Angeles. The Skybar opened in 1996 and soon became one of the LA glitterati's most high-profile destinations. Outsized pots and wooden divans decorate the bar, which is a celebration of the West Coast's outdoor, sun-worshipping lifestyle

Bar	Skybar
Hotel	Mondrian
Address	8440 Sunset Boulevard, Los Angeles, CA 90069, USA
Telephone	+1 323 650 8999
Opening hours	Mon–Sun 11am–2am
Number of seats	100
Design style	Tin-roofed, open-air hut with traditional American school house- and courthouse-style armchairs and bar stools
Clientele	The beautiful people. Not as exclusive as it once was, but still full of film industry types. The Miami equivalent at the Shore Club is more for music makers – Beyoncé, Jay-Z and so on
Speciality drinks/cocktails	Apple martinis
Music	No DJs
Membership details/ door policy	Still popular enough to require a selective door policy. Some movers and shakers have a pass key to ensure entry to the South Beach equivalent

Left: Mondrian, Los Angeles. The hotel lobby features Philippe Starck's careful placement of provocative objects and furniture

Opposite: The Shore Club, Miami. Philippe Starck adapted the idea of the Mondrian Skybar for the Shore Club when it was taken over by Ian Schrager. However, the design is very different with great emphasis on a central indoor area, the RedRoom, where lanterns and crimson lacquer are used to evoke Morocco

Below: The Shore Club, Miami. The swimming pool at the Skybar, with the RumBar's furnished, private lounges in the pergola. The huge, exclusive pool and bar complex has helped to reinvigorate South Beach as a celebrity hang-out

Above: **The Shore Club, Miami.** The lantern-filled pergola at the Skybar's RumBar, which features a choice of 75 rums

Right: **The Shore Club, Miami.** Colourful day beds decorate the side of the pool at the Skybar

Opposite: **The Shore Club, Miami.** The Skybar's garden is furnished with oversized cushions, taking the RedRoom's Moroccan theme outdoors

Met Bar, The Metropolitan Hotel

United Designers

Location: London
Completion date: 1997

When the Met Bar opened in 1997 it was something of a mould-breaker, leading the way for a new breed of exclusive bars. That a mere hotel, a type of institution famous for the vapidity of its bar design, had the nerve to have a members- and residents-only policy (enforced by clipboard Hitlers whose steely appraisal made a mere mortal's bones rattle) was shocking. A-list celebrities flooded in, emboldened by the protective door policy and enticed by a cool design that finally matched their own self-esteem. The Met Bar's reputation and media buzz have lasted almost a decade, but in truth the 'celebrities' are working their way down the alphabet and it's now hard to see from the interior design what all the fuss was about. However, that's more to do with how rapidly the culture of hotel and members' bars has developed, in terms of both the number of establishments and the quality of their design. Hopefully, the 2004 redesign of the bar will help this original jewel of the hotel-bar scene to re-establish itself.

The design for the hotel, by Keith Hobbs and Linzi Coppick of United Designers, is Minimalist, clean and contemporary. The glass panel suspended over the entrance, the white exterior, the sloping frame of the ground-floor window and the lower-case logo with its stretched ascenders let you know that you are entering a pure, unfussy world. Inside, the light-filled lobby is full of natural colours and materials, rounded shapes and pared-down style, culminating in an achingly cool, stress-free simplicity. The Helen Yardley carpet is abstract and unthreatening while the Armani uniforms worn by the staff are understated.

The Met Bar itself is only a cousin to the contemplative world of the rest of the hotel. It would have been difficult to match Minimalism to the decadent intentions of the proposed clientele, so the designers wisely strayed into a more exuberant palette. Stylistic detachment is enforced by street access directly into the ground-floor bar. Following the recent refit, the muted carpet, the round, brown leather armchairs that form petals around the white tables in the central space, and the odd organic curve of plasterwork, echo the natural shapes and materials in other parts of the hotel, but the bar counter has a more vibrant theme. The shining red surface of its top arcs out into the space above a corrugated silver frontage. The leather of the futuristic bar stools is also red, and this is the dominant colour around the sides of the bar, with red banquettes and low stools providing the main seating under a huge artwork. The banquettes curve slightly to suggest booths, while their backs share the corrugated theme of the bar-counter frontage.

The Met Bar seems dated despite its refurbishment (anything with futuristic elements always looks as though it was conceived in the 1950s), but some of its old confidence has returned. It is still subject to the slings and arrows that inevitably accompany a waning of hipness, a passing of the *Zeitgeist*, but its influence has been long standing and international. Owners and designers of the latest successful hotel bars, such as Q! The Bar in Berlin and INK in Singapore, continue to cite the Met as one of their primary influences; and Como Hotels, who own the hotel, have taken the entire Metropolitan concept to Bangkok.

Opposite: **Metropolitan, London.** The Met Bar was a new synthesis of hotel bar and private members' club. The red top of the bar counter sweeps out into the room, while the corrugations on its silver frontage are mirrored by the red banquettes against the far wall

Bar	Met Bar
Hotel	The Metropolitan
Address	Old Park Lane, Mayfair, London W1Y 4LB, UK
Telephone	+44 (0)20 7447 5757
Opening hours	Mon–Sat 11am–3.30am, Sun 11am–10.30pm
Capacity	150 including standing
Design style	Touches of futurism and Minimalism
Clientele	Stylish hotel guests. Still popular with 'celebrities', but these days the definition of the word has to be at its widest
Speciality drinks/cocktails	Extensive cocktail list; particularly strong on martinis
Music	DJs play lounge
Membership details/ door policy	Members and hotel guests only after 6pm

Left: Metropolitan, London. The centre of the bar features brown leather chairs, but the colour scheme is dominated by the huge red canvas and red banquettes. The use of red contrasts with the natural hues in the rest of the hotel

Below: Metropolitan, London. The hotel overlooks Hyde Park on Old Park Lane in Mayfair, which features a congregation of London's older, luxury hotels. When the Metropolitan opened in February 1997 it was the first new hotel on Park Lane for over 20 years and offered up-to-date technological facilities

Right: **Metropolitan, London.** Floor plan of bedrooms. Owner Christina Ong's directive to United Designers was to 'start with a clean sheet of paper and design a hotel to meet the needs and desires of the modern traveller'. Simplicity and pared-down elegance became central elements in the design

Below: **Metropolitan, London.** Clean lines, and natural shapes and materials, create a calm, subdued hotel-lobby area

Soho House New York

Ilse Crawford/Harman Jablin Architects

Location: New York
Completion date: 2003

The original Soho House opened in London in 1998, and soon became a fashionable private members' club and media hangout that was bracketed with the Groucho in terms of prestige. Like the Groucho, it was loosely connected to the traditional remit of a club, in providing social areas, club rooms and accommodation for an exclusive membership but, with its design and facilities more geared towards contemporary concepts of decadence and comfort, it offered a very modern twist.

Bringing the concept of an exclusive drinking den to New York was a different matter. The United States has always had a culture of members' clubs, but these have largely been rooted in sporting or alumni organisations rather than the creative decadence that is the stamp of the new English breed. The concept of exclusivity is one that does not sit as easily in the 'land of the free' as it does in Britain where social hierarchies are fading but still ingrained. To top this, New Yorkers are rightly proud of their distinctive bar and club culture and might have bristled at the thought of postcolonial limeys bringing their new, elitist model into the heart of the city's hip meat-packing district. Yet Soho House New York, a six-storey, 4180-square-metre (45,000-square-foot) former electrical warehouse converted by Harman Jablin Architects, has been a great success – and not only with ex-pat Brits. A measure of its status came soon after it opened, when an episode of 'Sex and the City' featured Samantha being denied access to its roof-top pool.

One of the main reasons for this success was the appointment as designer of Ilse Crawford, who worked with Soho House's owner Nick Jones on Babington House in Somerset, the acclaimed reinvention of the British country club. Founder and former editor of *Elle Decoration*, Crawford has always had an unnerving ability to determine what's in and what's out, which has led to her unfortunate 'lifestyle guru' tag. However, when it came to the Soho House venture, her real skill was in her understanding that, above all, members would want a genuine feeling of comfort mixed with a sense of style and luxury. Any idea of a rigid doctrine of contemporary style went out of the window, and Crawford created an atmosphere in which guests could have a dream apartment with no responsibilities – somewhere to relax in private. The result is eclectic, morphic interiors that mix European decadence with the rough edges that New Yorkers like to revel in.

The drawing room, one of the principal social areas of the club, says it all. Its rough brickwork and warehouse style are in sharp contrast to the refined, panelled ceiling, while the furniture ranges from stuffed leather armchairs to low, sci-fi pods with cutaway sections. The library may have red leather seating, but its walls are decorated with Deborah Bowness' custom-made bookshelf-wallpaper and the ceiling beams are exposed. The resident media hotshots can enjoy elitist luxury without thinking they've sold their souls to the devil or lost touch with the real New York.

Crawford makes some witty references to English club culture, particularly with 12-metre (39-foot), 'stretched limo' chesterfields in the bar, but, importantly, there is no suggestion that Brits are subduing the New York sense of adventure with an overbearing, traditional dogma. It seems to be a happy marriage.

Opposite: **Soho House New York.** The club is an eclectic mix of styles from across the ages. The loft-style drawing room, one of its major social areas, features futuristic pod chairs and cylindrical tables alongside vintage furniture and old-fashioned leather sofas

Club	Soho House New York
Address	29–35 Ninth Avenue, New York, NY 10014, USA
Telephone	+1 212 627 9800
Opening hours	Mon–Thurs, Sun 11am–3am, Fri–Sat 11am–4am
Design style	New York loft meets English club and European retro
Clientele	Fashion Brits Alexander McQueen and Stella McCartney have been guests, while *Vogue*'s Anna Wintour held a party here for the Beckhams. Harvey Weinstein and Graydon Carter are founder members
Speciality drinks/cocktails	Ginger martinis
Music	Not really a music destination
Membership details/ door policy	Members only ($1100 pa, with $200 registration fee), but hotel guests can use the facilities.

Below: **Soho House New York**. The library mixes the stylish, the rough and the witty. Beneath the exposed ceiling beams, furniture by George Smith, B&B Italia and Arne Jacobsen is surrounded by Deborah Bowness' faux-library wallpaper

Right: **Soho House New York.** The 24 hotel rooms are split into different types. The Play House features Studio Ilse's wall stencils, George Smith's chesterfield and an oversized anglepoise lamp by Twentytwentyone

Below: **Soho House New York.** The Play House rooms mix the ornate and the Minimalist, with carved bedsteads and egg-shaped baths in the bedrooms

Above: Soho House London. The original Soho House London opened in 1998 and there is a waiting list to join it. The bar is the pivotal space, with buttoned leather banquettes standing out against brown and white floral wallpaper. The centre of the room is dominated by the semicircular bar counter

Below: Soho House London. Like the New York venture with its top-storey pool, the original Soho House makes use of the building's height with a roof-deck bar that leads on to a terrace overlooking the busy streets of Soho

Opposite: Soho House London. The dining room features a long wooden table, oak floors and leather-panelled walls

Below: Soho House London. The room called 'the Library' is a throwback to traditional gentlemen's clubs, but it is a versatile space for private meetings, lunches and dinners rather than a repository for books

Morrison Bar, Morrison

Douglas Wallace with John Rocha as design consultant

Location: Dublin
Completion date: 1999

Architects and designers Douglas Wallace converted an 18th-century Georgian town house overlooking the Liffey into one of the major, modern luxury hotels in Ireland. The original facade was left more or less intact, but is now incorporated within a purpose-built, ultramodern hotel. The owner Hugh O'Regan worked closely with Hugh Wallace and added fashion designer John Rocha into the mix to help Dublin hotel architecture take a great leap forward. The quasi-Minimalist design manages to combine a sense of Eastern spiritualism, the starkness of a contemporary art gallery and an Irish love of warmth and comfort. Thankfully for the locals, the last quality is the most prevalent in the much admired Morrison Bar.

The bar is very contemporary with sharp angles and light-coloured walls, but it is dominated by natural tones and materials, including stained woods, and leather and suede, while the lighting is discreet. The space is geared towards comfort, with custom-made armchairs, bar stools by Tadhg and Simon O'Driscoll, and relaxing sofas. There is also a sense of openness as the room flows freely into the café on the same level, while the bar's large windows make it something of a showpiece for passers-by. The design may be understated, as if it has been consciously drawn back from being too zealously pretentious, but the Morrison Bar remains a glamorous place in which to see and be seen.

The sense of international adventure and Eastern influence is more obvious at Lobo, the hotel's late-night bar and Asian restaurant. The communal space between the bar and restaurant features a series of dramatic statements including the prominent placing of a huge, Africanesque wooden head by Irish sculptor Eoin Byrne. A similarly oversized golden gong dominates one end of the room, and is complemented by yellow, underbar lighting. Much of the seating, including the bar stools and poufs, is covered in white leather, with the odd splash of red material, while the inebriated have the option of red, bed-like loungers. As a result, Lobo manages to be both highly stylised and decadent. It may be geared to attract a celebrity-heavy, international clientele, but, like the Morrison Bar, it provides a fitting backdrop to the new-found creative and business confidence that has spurred on Dublin youth in recent years.

The lobby of the Morrison gives a strong sense of what lies at the heart of this design adventure. Its long, narrow strip of grey and cream carpet at first seems to be abstract, or in some way related to feng shui. In truth, it is an evocation of the Liffey River that runs alongside the hotel. The Morrison appears to be full of Eastern promise, but its soul really belongs to a very Celtic tiger.

Left: Morrison, Dublin. The careful, symmetrical placing of objects is a feature throughout the hotel, and is carried through to the Morrison Bar which is decorated with vases standing in rectangular, yellow recesses. The stained-oak bar stools are by Tadhg and Simon O'Driscoll

Opposite: Morrison, Dublin. The Morrison Bar has a reputation for being both cool and comfortable. Dark wooden floors, discreet lighting, and a mix of cream and dark leather armchairs ensure that even though the bar has a very contemporary and glamorous feel, it is also understated and welcoming in a way that appeals to local regulars

Bar	Morrison Bar
Hotel	Morrison
Address	Lower Ormond Quay, Dublin 1, Ireland
Telephone	+353 (0)1 887 2400
Opening hours	Mon–Wed, Sun 10.30am–11.30pm, Thurs–Sat 10.30am–12.30pm
Number of seats	100
Design style	East meets West while somehow remaining thoroughly Irish
Clientele	Kylie Minogue was an early guest at the Morrison, while Robbie Williams has graced the bar, but the hard core are local film and media types
Speciality drinks/cocktails	For a touch of Irish flavour, the Pink Cloud is made of Smirnoff vanilla, Baileys and fresh strawberry purée
Music	Mostly pop. Go downstairs to Lobo to get funky
Membership details/ door policy	Popularity means there is a selective night-time doorman, so you'd better look the part

Above: **Morrison, Dublin.** As well as the huge gong, Lobo is dominated by a huge carved head by the Irish sculptor Eoin Byrne

Below: **Morrison, Dublin.** The variety of largely white seats in Lobo is broken up by red beds that offer a touch of decadence

Above: **Morrison, Dublin.** Lobo's Eastern theme is borne out by the huge, golden gong that dominates the end of the space. The bar is dressed with the same O'Driscoll stools as the Morrison Bar, but with the addition of a white, natural leather, back support

Above: **Morrison, Dublin.** Reflecting its East meets West theme, the hotel also has a fusion restaurant, the Halo. The dark wooden tables and pale chairs of the lower level are cupped in the sweeping, wooden curve that separates the main sections

Below: **Morrison, Dublin.** The Penthouse apartment features the hotel's characteristic whites, browns and blacks with delicate Eastern touches

Light Bar, St Martin's Lane

Philippe Starck

Location: London
Completion date: 1999

It is hard to recall the level of shock that greeted the opening of the St Martin's Lane in London in September 1999. A seemingly ordinary 1960s building, whose only distinction was to house the much-loved Lumiere cinema in an otherwise unnoticeable office block, had been transformed into a hotel unlike anything the city had seen before.

The surprises at the St Martin's Lane begin outside, where Philippe Starck's interior plays with the perceptions of passers-by. The design is inspired by light and its motivation is fun. Guests can control the colour of the lighting in their rooms, so from outside, when the full-length windows are lit, the facade looks like a multicoloured chequerboard. On the ground floor, the glazed entranceway is disconcerting. On either side of the revolving door, gauze curtains block most of the view of the interior – only the bottom third is visible. Passers-by have an enticing glimpse of an unusual world. Stooping, it is possible to see the fluorescent yellow glow of the walls, odd sculptural forms and people's feet; but the focal point is a simple doorway, glowing with light, directly across the lobby. This is the Light Bar and the journey to it begins on the pavement outside.

Inside the bar, past indifferent hostesses with clipboards, the hotel's light theme reaches its zenith. The long, narrow space is made up of four 'rooms', marked out by different colours of saturated light: pink, violet, green and orange. Everything within each 'room' is either painted, covered or lit in the same colour, so there are four specific, monochrome worlds – to walk the length of the bar is to travel halfway through a rainbow. From the entranceway the space seems low, but each room rises to over 6 metres (20 feet), with huge, close-up photographs of highly expressive faces, taken by Jean Baptiste Mondino, decorating the walls above normal ceiling height. Small tables with etched colour-glass tops are surrounded by chrome framed-chairs and suede banquettes that match the room's colour. Surprisingly, the bar counter is not the focal point of the Light Bar; instead, the eye is drawn to a glimmering, candle-lit glass display at the end of the space.

To begin with, the bar was a huge popular success but a logistical failure. Quite simply, the relationship between the height of the chairs and the tables meant that customers kept on knocking their drinks over. The furniture was changed. In the end, despite all their artful surprises, Schrager and Starck have a very pragmatic streak and want their hotels to work on a simple, practical level.

The key to getting to grips with the best elements of the Schrager/Starck liaison is understanding the possibly complex reactions their designs inspire, rather than just looking at the inventory. The careful play of light, the peculiar placement of oversized and undersized objects, the mix and match of traditions – these are all there either to make connections, or to surprise, on a very personal level. If their designs evoke nothing beyond what you can see, then they have failed.

Left: St Martin's Lane, London. Guests can control the colour of the lighting in their rooms, which have floor-to-ceiling windows. At night, the exterior of the building becomes a grid of different colours

Opposite: St Martin's Lane, London. Revolving doors in traditional hotels often act as a barrier to what lies beyond, but at the St Martin's Lane Hotel they are clear glass, and provide the only unobscured view into the lobby and the Light Bar directly opposite

Bar	Light Bar
Hotel	St Martin's Lane
Address	45 St Martin's Lane, London WC2N 4HX, UK
Telephone	+44 (0)20 7300 5500
Opening hours	Mon–Sat 5.30pm–3am, Sun 5.30pm–1am
Number of seats	60
Design style	Innovative colour-saturated niches adorned on high by Jean Baptiste Mondino's photographs of amusing faces
Clientele	Hotel guests, media movers and shakers
Speciality drinks/cocktails	Passionfruit martinis
Music	DJ Thurs–Sat
Membership details/ door policy	So popular that it's still reserved for hotel residents and those on the guest list unless you get there early

Above, left: **St Martin's Lane, London.** The lobby has an array of carefully arranged, eclectic pieces that often cross the line between furniture and art

Above, right: **St Martin's Lane, London.** Surrounded by the roof tops of Covent Garden, the Penthouse and Apartment suites have custom-designed furniture by Philippe Starck

Opposite: **St Martin's Lane, London.** The Light Bar is split into four distinct monochrome zones in which all the fixtures and fittings match that section's colour. Each 'room' rises into a surprising shaft adorned with Jean Baptiste Mondino's close-up photographs of expressive faces

Right: **St Martin's Lane, London.** The hotel's Asia de Cuba restaurant features low-hanging, naked light-bulbs and large columns bedecked with revolving exhibits

MINK, Prince of Wales

Wayne Finschi

Location: Melbourne
Completion date: 1997

The Prince of Wales, more usually known as 'the Prince', was a crumbling Art Deco ruin before it was taken over in 1996 by Frank and John van Haandel, who set about restoring it and establishing a new hotel complex with bars and restaurants. The St Kilda area of Melbourne was starting to be transformed into a desirable destination and the renovation of the Prince of Wales would meet the demands of the new clientele. By the time the 40-room boutique hotel was completed in 1999 MINK, one of the new bars that had been opened two years earlier, was already something of a celebrity haunt. Its fame and popularity do not seem to have diminished in the intervening years and it is now an Australian institution.

Designer Wayne Finschi worked with the van Haandel brothers to convert the Prince's underground, former pool hall. The result is a decadent vodka bar that has its velvet-draped heart firmly ensconced in the Cold War. The yellow walls of the main room are broken up by a cartoon-like wall painting by local artist Marcus Davidson. This originally decorated the pool hall and has been incorporated in the Russian theme with the addition of Cyrillic script proclaiming the space to be the 'People's Café'. Trim, red leather banquettes are suspended from wall fixings and small, wooden chairs make up the rest of the seating, accompanied by square, plain or round, silver-edged tables. The main bar still has a slightly Art Deco feel, but this disappears in the hallway, which continues the yellow and red theme and features the occasional Russian mural.

The bar really comes into its own in its small alcoves and lounges, which are inspired by the Trans-Siberian Express and are available for exclusive hire. Luscious, blue velvet curtains conceal the sexy, red-lit interiors of the alcoves, each of which is adorned with a sensual wall painting that suggests Russians know how to keep warm. The front lounge, its entrance dressed by red velvet curtains, has dark, half-panelled walls and smart, roll-backed, red leather banquettes beneath a collage of Supremacist posters. The Russian theme extends to the food menu and a freezer cabinet with over 40 vodkas, while a range of Cuban cigars is also on offer.

Each aspect of the Prince has its own identity. In contrast to MINK, the bar attached to Circa – one of Melbourne's most acclaimed restaurants – is an elegant, almost delicate cocktail bar. Amid the pink shock of the carpet and bar-stool seats, the tables and chairs stand on the thinnest possible supports. The bar counter itself is also slender and has soft, glowing underlighting. Conversely, the Public Bar downstairs has been preserved to attract the more rough-and-ready crowd that was the backbone of both the St Kilda area and the Prince of Wales before each underwent a more rarefied transformation.

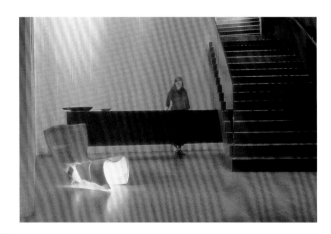

Opposite: **Prince of Wales, Melbourne.** The run-down Art Deco building has been converted into nine ventures, including a 40-room boutique hotel, several restaurants and bars, and a spa. St Kilda, a seaside suburb of Melbourne, always had a slightly raucous reputation but is becoming known as a more sophisticated destination

Left: **Prince of Wales, Melbourne.** The spaciousness, artistic surprises and use of gauze curtains make the hotel foyer reminiscent of the work of Philippe Starck

Bar	MINK
Hotel	Prince of Wales
Address	2b Acland Street, St Kilda, Melbourne 3182, Australia
Telephone	+61 (0)3 9536 1199
Opening hours	Mon–Thurs 6pm–2am, Fri–Sun 6pm–3am
Capacity	120 seated plus 100 standing
Design style	Russian-inspired velvet underground
Clientele	Broad range of locals, tourists and the odd celeb. Cate Blanchett is said to have been a fan
Speciality drinks/cocktails	Vodka cocktails including the Long Cool One (featuring cucumber-infused Absolut, Pimms and Grand Marnier
Music	Mellow jazz early in the week gives way to the latest house on Sundays
Membership details/door policy	None

Above: **Prince of Wales, Melbourne.** MINK's long hallway is reminiscent of a train carriage

Above: **Prince of Wales, Melbourne.** Circa, the Prince's award-winning restaurant, is an elegant, bright, white creation overlooking Port Phillip Bay. Sheer black and pink drapes grace the walls while woven wicker cones are hung low from the ceiling

Below: **Prince of Wales, Melbourne.** A partial cartoon-like artwork on the walls of MINK's main room dates back to the bar's life as a pool hall

Below: **Prince of Wales, Melbourne.** MINK's lounges can be booked for exclusive use. A collage of Russian posters adorns the half-panelled walls of the front one. Velvet curtains, red lamp-shades and red leather banquettes suggest this is going to be a very hot Cold War

Above: **Prince of Wales, Melbourne.** The different areas of the complex are stylistically distinct. The Circa cocktail bar is full of contemporary art, delicate furniture and vibrant colours

Above: **Prince of Wales, Melbourne.** The underground vodka bar MINK is inspired by the Trans-Siberian Express. Plush materials, Russian murals and secret liaisons in hidden alcoves are the order of the day

Lobby Bar, One Aldwych

Gordon Campbell Gray with Mary Fox-Linton

Location: London
Completion date: 1998

The ridiculously award-laden One Aldwych seems to feature in almost every list of the best hotels in London, Europe and the world. Importantly, as it is situated on the cusp between the business district of the City and the entertainment-heavy West End, it scores highly as both a business and leisure hotel. It does not appeal only to travellers: its two restaurants, coffee bar and, especially, the Lobby Bar are extremely popular with Londoners. When it opened in 1998, the bar soon established itself at the forefront of the hotels that were becoming recognised as stylish, cocktail destinations.

One Aldwych has the advantage of being in a curvaceous, dome-topped, triangular building that is a highlight of London's remaining Edwardian architecture. It was built in 1907 by the leading hotel architects Mewès & Davis, who designed the Ritz hotels in Paris and London, but was initially the offices of the Morning Post newspaper. The building spent time as a bank before its new owner Gordon Campbell Gray decided to belatedly, but fittingly, turn the Mewès & Davis design into a luxury hotel. The facade, which is partially clad in Norwegian granite, combines an Edwardian concept of classicism with typically Parisian ornamentation, including decorative ironwork, balustrades and garland swags, all of which suit the building's new function. The interior, under the guidance of Campbell Gray's creative inspiration, is a mixture of contemporary and classic styles that appeals to both the luxury traveller and the London cognoscenti.

The Lobby Bar, which inhabits much of the ground floor, is in what was the newspaper's advertisement hall. Visitors are met by a contemporary, sparkling, steel-mesh wall, but this gives way to the classic grandeur of double-height ceilings, tall windows and oak panelling. The limestone floor and white, ribbed pillars help to emphasise the airiness of the space, which leads to a dark, arcing bar. All the furniture, which again combines the contemporary with the more old-fashioned, has been custom-designed, including the stately, incredibly high-backed chairs in the street-side windows. Much of the furniture in the centre of the room consists of miniature armchairs gathered around small, wooden tables. The hotel has an art collection of several hundred contemporary works including, in the bar area, André Wallace's large wooden sculpture *The Boatman*; the figure raises his oars into the air as if to say that he, too, has finished his work for the day.

The continued success of the Lobby Bar has been helped by the quality of its hot and cold food, which has an organic slant, and its range of cocktails. Its tamarillo martini was named 'Best Cocktail in London' by *Forbes* magazine in 2004. Another popular bar is attached to the hotel's Axis restaurant.

Left: One Aldwych, London.
The double-height space of the Lobby Bar is light, airy and grand. Oversized, high-backed chairs sit in the huge windows to the left of the bar

Opposite: One Aldwych, London.
Designed by Mewès & Davis, the architects of the Ritz hotels in London and Paris, the Edwardian exterior of the triangular building has ornate, Parisian decoration. Like the Ritz in Piccadilly, it's one of London's earliest examples of a steel-framed building

Bar	Lobby Bar
Hotel	One Aldwych
Address	1 Aldwych, London WC2B 4RH, UK
Telephone	+44 (0)20 7300 1000
Opening hours	Mon–Fri 8am–11pm, Sat 9am–11pm, Sun 10am–11.30pm
Capacity	60 plus 40 standing
Design style	Grand Edwardian hall with contemporary art and furniture
Clientele	Smart and affluent guests mingle with mix of businesspeople and after-work crowd
Speciality drinks/cocktails	40 martinis, including the tamarillo, fig and Below Passion
Music	Classical
Membership details/ door policy	None

Right: One Aldwych, London. The very popular, buzzing Lobby Bar, as seen from the balcony

Below: One Aldwych, London. The hotel has a collection of 350 contemporary artworks, including André Wallace's *The Boatman*

Above: **One Aldwych, London.** One Aldwych features two restaurants, including the Axis where one wall is dominated by explosive, skyscraper shards

Below: **One Aldwych, London.** High wooden stools stand before the polished sheen of the bar counter. The Lobby Bar is a popular cocktail destination for Londoners as well as tourists

Above: **One Aldwych, London.** Elegance and luxury are the keys to the design of the hotel's 105 suites and rooms

Blue Bar, Bleibtreu

Herbert J Weinand

Location: Berlin
Completion date: 1995

Bleibtreu may look like a sedate town house on a quiet, elegant Kurfürstendamm street lined with upmarket boutiques, but it masks what was in 1995 a very modern concept of an urban, youthful, multifunctional eco-hotel. Its frontage includes a popular, Italian-style espresso bar, an artistic florist and a New York-style delicatessen, all of which reveal Bleibtreu's desire to be part of the local fabric of the area and offer an experience beyond that of a normal hotel. Further in towards the entrance is the very cool, chill-out zone of the Blue Bar and Restaurant 31 – two of its major focal points.

At first the hotel seems to be something of an addendum to these leisure areas, as it only really reveals itself through a courtyard of blue pebbles that hints at the interior's major themes. The reception area itself is as small as possible: Bleibtreu has more interesting experiences to offer than lounging in a lobby. Away from this crowded spot, the rest of the hotel is light and airy, with a glass lift that travels through tree branches and a general emphasis on natural, oatmeal and blue tones.

Almost everything in Bleibtreu, which translates as 'stay true', was specifically designed by Herbert J Weinand and crafted in either Italy or Germany, so nothing about it feels prepackaged. Each item, from the chemical-free paint, untreated oak furniture and virgin-wool carpets to the organic food and beverages, has been made to high, ecologically friendly standards. However, this is not a step into the past. The Bleibtreu looks towards a technologically savvy future, with remote-controlled dimmer lights in its rooms reflecting its ambition to be part of an advanced, comfortable and ecological environment. Beyond the eco-friendly fixtures and fittings 'wellness' has an important role to play, with a range of health and beauty treatments on offer in the relaxation centre and sugar-free food in the restaurant.

Fittingly for a cool, urban chill-out bar, the Blue Bar is darker and moodier than the rest of the hotel. Its name, which is written large and as if slightly distorted by water in a wall recess, gives the game away. Light-blue walls surround darker blue furniture, creating an underwater world that is disturbed only by the yellow lighting that comes through from the adjoining spaces, including Restaurant 31. The sofas and stools feature seats with folded end-rolls atop wooden rostra. The clear glass table-tops, which also sit on similar wooden frames, and the abstract carpet and marble floor evoke the sea, but the design carries with it a very German industrialism. Much of the hotel may be about the preservation of the planet, but the Blue Bar is as good a place as any in which to self-destruct on too many cocktails. However, anyone who does not want to let their feeling of wellness ebb away can order a vitamin cocktail instead.

The Ku'Damm is starting to be known as a nightlife – as well as a shopping – destination. As can be said of much of Bleibtreu, the Blue Bar was ahead of its time.

Opposite: **Bleibtreu, Berlin.** The hotel is on a quiet, elegant street lined with boutiques in the Ku'Damm area of Berlin

Opposite: **Bleibtreu, Berlin.** The Blue Bar lives up to its name. It's an underwater experience, relieved only by light from the adjoining spaces

Bar	Blue Bar
Hotel	Bleibtreu
Address	Bleibtreustrasse 31, 10707 Berlin, Germany
Telephone	+49 (0)30 884 74 0
Opening hours	8am–midnight
Number of seats	30
Design style	Small, underwater chill-out room
Clientele	Increasingly trendy Ku'Damm locals
Speciality drinks/cocktails	Cocktails, from classic to vitamin
Music	Chill-out, lounge
Membership details/ door policy	None

Above: Bleibtreu, Berlin. Restaurant 31 is an acclaimed, ecologically friendly restaurant that overlooks the hotel courtyard. It celebrates organic shapes as well as organic food, and features mosaic pillars decorated as strata

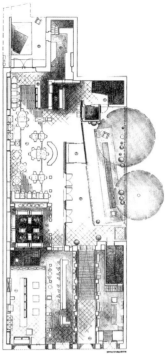

Above: **Bleibtreu, Berlin.** Ground-floor plan of the hotel, with the small, square Blue Bar in the middle

Above: **Bleibtreu, Berlin.** The reception area is across the blue-pebbled courtyard

MyBar, MyHotel

Conran & Partners

Location: London
Completion date: 1999

MyHotel refers to itself as a new breed of hotel, and its bar fits well into the new breed of London drinking establishments that took root in the late 1990s. In recent years, Conran & Partners has undertaken high-profile Japanese projects that combine a Western design sensibility with Eastern culture, but in 1999 they were already developing this philosophical/structural syncopation on the edge of Bloomsbury, the symbol of sophisticated, literary London. The hotel is on a small road that joins the quiet of Bedford Square to Tottenham Court Road with its bustling chaos of pile-'em-high discount electrical shops. A few yards away, MyHotel is a calm oasis that was inspired by the owner's interest in Eastern values.

The hotel is personal and modern, while offering a tranquillity that is emphasised by the designers' adherence to feng shui with its interplay between the seen and unseen – implemented here through the careful placement of objects that create a balance between opposites. The interior consists of an internal street that links the main public areas. The reception lies to the left and features a freestanding, curved counter covered with leather and dark wood. This mirrors the bar counter, which is immediately visible through a pair of black-framed doorways to the right. It is exactly the same shape as the reception desk but is clad in pale wood and features a zinc top. Set into the party wall between the reception and bar there is a fish tank through which the adjacent space can be glimpsed.

Inside the bar, the colours are muted greys and browns – part of the design may have its roots in the East, but MyBar could easily have been transported from New York. Brown leather chairs and white marble-topped tables line the narrow strip of the main room, which opens out on to the pavement in summer, giving a New York-deli feel to the space during the day. At night, the bar's mood and clientele change considerably. It becomes an urban crush of cocktail drinkers and the back snug comes into its own. Mirrors, grey curtains and brown banquettes line the walls of this small room to create a sophisticated, private den. Instead of the veined white marble in the main bar, the table tops are a thick-grained wood veneer. Whether you admire feng-shui principles or snigger at them, MyBar is a successful contemporary bar in an awkward space, and, for all the philosophy, it exudes less misplaced design 'attitude' than many other places.

MyHotel also has a restaurant. Behind the reception area, this is dominated by a straight line of tables down the centre of the room, which can be pushed together to form a refectory table. Accommodation is reached via a red-leather-clad lift designed to make guests feel as though they are being transported inside a piece of luggage.

Since the success of MyHotel in Bloomsbury, the enterprise has expanded to include other, individually designed hotels including MyHotel Chelsea, which is described as '"Brideshead Revisited" meets "Sex and the City"', and the prospective MyHotel Brighton, to be designed by Karim Rashid.

Opposite: **MyHotel, London.** The canopy-covered entrance to MyHotel in Bloomsbury, the first of the MyHotel chain, leads to an East–West fusion of design

Bar	MyBar
Hotel	MyHotel
Address	11–13 Bayley Street, London WC1B 3HD, UK
Telephone	+44 (0)20 7667 6000
Opening hours	Open to guests 24 hours a day. Food served 11am–11pm
Number of seats	40
Design style	Eastern concepts blended with intimate New York café-bar style
Clientele	Particularly popular with local 30-somethings who like stylish bars but no longer feel they need to try too hard
Speciality drinks/cocktails	Freshly blended cocktails
Music	No live music or DJs
Membership details/ door policy	None

Above: **MyHotel, London.** The focal point of the narrow main space in MyBar is the floating, zinc-topped bar counter. Most of the chairs are brown leather, with a variety of coloured armchairs towards the rear

Right: **MyHotel, London.** MyBar can be glimpsed through the black-framed doorway and the fish tank in the reception area

Above: MyHotel, London. MyBar's back room is an intimate, grey-curtained snug. Unlike the rest of the bar, it is only really suited to night-time escapades

Right: MyHotel, London. A lounge and bedroom in the hotel, whose design features a blend of Western luxury and Eastern philosophy

ECQ Bar, Quay Grand Suites

Mirvac

Location: Sydney
Completion date: 1999

Central areas of Barcelona were tremendously reinvigorated by the investment linked to the city's hosting of the Olympic Games in 1992, and the legacy has been enduring, helping to establish Barcelona as one of Europe's entertainment and cultural capitals. Capturing the Olympics has become more than a matter of pride: with the right type of investment in infrastructure, the long-term financial gains can outstrip the incredible cost of the initial outlay.

Sydney 2000 was the biggest and most successful Olympic Games on record, and the fillip it gave to the tourism industry and the effect it had in redeveloping sectors of the city has been enormous – none more so than in East Circular Quay. In the years leading up to the Olympics the development of the area – close to the Sydney Opera House and several other important historical sites – was controversial and tortuous. The resulting main complex is disparagingly referred to by locals as 'the toaster', but the development survived the various divisions and compromises to become a new style quarter with a range of restaurants, bars, boutiques and the Quay Grand Suites hotel.

Since it opened in 1999 Quay Grand Suites has become Mirvac Hotels and Resort's flagship hotel. The group's parent company, Mirvac Developments Pty Ltd, itself undertook its development and the design of the building and its interior. Unusually, the expensive but highly rated accommodation consists entirely of suites, each with a separate living/dining area and kitchen. One of the most alluring features of the hotel's location is its views of Sydney Harbour, including the bridge, the opera house and the Royal Botanical Gardens, and the development makes the most of this. The regeneration of the area also means that the hotel is ideally situated to provide popular social spaces that appeal to a local clientele as well as hotel guests. The ECQ Bar is on the mezzanine level, with views directly across the harbour.

The aura of the bar is graceful and calm. The long, wood-clad counter has an elegant marble surround, while the internal walls are also white, creating a very light space. The décor is swish, clean and modern with slim, white chairs and tables, and leather-covered chrome stools, adding to its sophistication. Naturally, though, this is an outward-looking space. The floor-to-ceiling windows make the most of the view and can be fully opened on to glass balconies. This gives the bar a sense of the outdoors and a feeling that it is right above the water. There is also a patio terrace with wicker furniture.

The ECQ Bar has played its part in an emerging re-evaluation of 'the toaster'. In the six years since Quay Grand Suites was completed, the Sydney bar scene has metamorphosised beyond recognition as the city has become more cosmopolitan in a European sense. This hotel bar, however, still remains a popular, but never raucous, favourite with local 30-somethings.

Opposite: **Quay Grand Suites, Sydney.** The emphasis in the ECQ Bar's interior is on light, stylish furniture and materials

Left: **Quay Grand Suites, Sydney.** The ECQ Bar makes the most of its view – including Sydney Harbour Bridge – with tinted floor-to-ceiling windows that can be folded back to leave a glass balcony as the only obstruction

Bar	ECQ Bar
Hotel	Quay Grand Suites
Address	East Circular Quay, 61 Macquarie Street, Sydney 2000, Australia
Telephone	+61 (0)2 9256 4000
Opening hours	Mon–Fri noon–midnight, Sat 1pm–midnight, Sun 1pm–9pm
Number of seats	100
Design style	Contemporary chic with great views
Clientele	Fashionable 30- to 40-somethings
Speciality drinks/cocktails	None. Classic cocktails include good margaritas
Music	Contemporary background
Membership details/ door policy	None

the establishment

The common perception of traditional luxury hotels and members' clubs is that both are adverse to change. After all, their longevity is tied up with providing a certain level of service in a setting that their largely conservative, wealthy clientele regards as stylish. Abandoning Louis XVI-style grandeur in favour of a John Pawsonesque Minimalism is bound to jeopardise an establishment's relationship with its core customers. It may lead to some much-needed, but altogether brief, coverage in the press but the effect of this can soon disappear, along with cherished regulars.

However, some hotel and club owners are conscious that their longevity can be sustained only if they have a relationship with a younger generation – one whose ideas of luxury are very different to those of their parents. They expect technological facilities to be provided – for some, paying a premium rate is allied to plasma screens and broadband connectivity. These elements can usually be incorporated into an existing scheme, albeit at some cost. The real challenge comes in dealing with the greater design expectations that are the result of the new wave of hotels and private members' clubs. It is not just that there is an ever-growing aversion to formality and chintz: the design must be out of the ordinary; it must delight, thrill and surprise.

The Establishment

The Commonwealth Club realised that its old stance and traditions could jeopardise its survival, and used design to reinvent itself completely. On the other hand its Victorian cousin, the Reform Club, has no problem sustaining itself and is aware that any reinvention would involve unnecessary risk. There are also places that are so entwined with the past that their history lies at their core. The Long Bar at Raffles in Singapore isn't merely a bit of twee, tourist nonsense – its new design is inspired by the style established by the plantation owners who created the bar in the first place. Its role is to preserve that memory of early Singapore while a wave of new hotel bars celebrates the city's architectural rebirth. Change would kill it.

Some of the projects in this chapter reflect a neat and economically viable way of sidestepping the issue of redevelopment. The Berkeley continues to offer its old-fashioned, conservative style of luxury, with the addition of new technology, but has allowed its social spaces to be reborn for the new, design-savvy consumer. And, like other establishments, it has found that improving the quality and design of its restaurants and bars in line with the new expectations about social space creates a relationship with the wider, money-laden community, and consequently doubles the benefits of a good, city location. The Blue Bar has reinvigorated the reputation of the Berkeley while the original clientele has been retained.

Traditional hotels and clubs with their often delicate fabrics, dated interior layouts and listed status are famously loath to take on the exorbitant costs of change. Redefining a bar in order to attract the knowledgeable, but inherently fickle, media mafia and fashionistas can mean joining a game of reinvention that has no end. Its designer must be supremely skilful at creating a progressive, innovative interior that will still delight and surprise in five years' time.

Below: **Commonwealth Club, London.** The 1997 redesign of the Commonwealth Club helped to change the outdated perception of the Royal Commonwealth Society and gave it a new lease of life

The Blue Bar, The Berkeley

David Collins

Location: London
Completion date: 1999

The Blue Bar at The Berkeley provides one of the best examples of a traditional hotel that has opened its doors to contemporary bar design while losing none of its finesse and formality. David Collins, who also masterminded the new bar at Claridge's, says: 'My brief was to establish a design concept that was in keeping with The Berkeley but with some contemporary vibe'. The 'vibe' is blue, and the result is a beautiful, striking room that retains some of its original features but places them in a compelling, fresh and witty context. It could seem to offer a monochromatic onslaught, but it is never overbearing.

The hotel has been established since the 19th century, but only moved to its current purpose-built home, designed by Martin O'Rourke, in 1972. Some of the original building's features also made the transition, most notably Sir Edwin Lutyens's wood panelling and carvings, which were placed in a sitting room. Formerly known as the Lutyens Room, this has become the Blue Bar.

Not many people would have taken its most notable feature – the intricate wall carvings – and covered them with blue paint, then had the nerve to emphasise what some would consider an art crime by naming the paint Lutyens Blue. The colour is reminiscent of Wedgwood, but red powder has been brushed into the cracked paint to prevent the space feeling too cool. The red is further picked out by the wall lights, and the surprising warmth of the room is reinforced by black leather flooring and the black frames of the lilac leather chairs.

Collins may be brave, but his decisions show depth and education. The light fitting in the decorated recess of the white ceiling is the 'Cardinal's Hat', Lutyens's creation for one of his famed country-house designs and the use of black is inspired by Sir Edwin's fondness for the colour.

The Blue Bar is a careful amalgamation of details. The onyx blade of the bar top, the sloping, square backs of the chairs, the blue-and-black rug and even the wide-rimmed, square ashtrays all give a nod to Art Deco, adding the glamour of the cocktail age to this faux-Renaissance setting.

Large convex mirrors, looking like studded shields or oversized portholes, provide a fish-eye view of the interior. Customers who catch their warped reflections see themselves among a diverse, well-heeled crowd of fashionistas, celebrities and casual drinkers in a place that manages to be intimate and formal, contemporary and timeless. It is said that Madonna has replicated the bar in her home.

The key to the longevity of the Blue Bar's popularity is that the décor is witty without being acerbic, and coolly stylish without a hint of desperation.

Opposite: **The Berkeley, London.** In the Blue Bar the intricacy of Sir Edwin Lutyens's wood wall-carvings still stands out in designer David Collins's study in blue. The onyx-topped bar is placed centrally at one end of the room, but the bottle displays are split into two recesses so that they do not detract from the drawing-room impression

Bar	The Blue Bar
Hotel	The Berkeley
Address	Wilton Place, Knightsbridge, London SW1X 7RL, UK
Telephone	+44 (0)20 7235 6000
Opening hours	4pm–1am
Number of seats	55
Design style	Opulent faux Renaissance meets contemporary chic
Clientele	Fashion crowd (it's John Galliano's 'home from home'), Sloanes, the rich and famous of Belgravia and visiting celebs
Speciality drinks/cocktails	The Berkeley champagne cocktail; Gingerpine Cosmo, a cosmopolitan with fresh ginger and ginger-infused vodka
Music	Has its own Blue Bar CD, an eclectic mix of dance, deep house, jazz and world music
Membership details/ door policy	No 'velvet rope' but once the bar reaches a certain level, VIPs & hotel guests have priority

Left: The Berkeley, London. The Berkeley moved from Mayfair to Martin O'Rourke's purpose-built premises in Knightsbridge in 1972. Fortunately, Lutyens's wood carvings and panelling were transported from the old building. Born in 1869, Lutyens remains famous for the Cenotaph in London, Castle Drogo in Devon and a range of significant country houses

Left: The Berkeley, London. The onyx table tops and bar surface help to break up the monochrome effect and provide some stylish textural variation. A Grape and Smoke menu matches particular wines with cigars – a contemporary twist on an old-world sensibility that is typical of the Blue Bar

Opposite: The Berkeley, London. The entrance to the five-star Berkeley remains formal and the open fire is enticing in winter. The shape of the wall lights in the Blue Bar is reminiscent of that of the exterior ones

Senso, Hôtel de la Trémoille

Conran & Partners

Location: Paris
Completion date: 2002

Hôtel de la Trémoille reopened in 2002 after an extensive refurbishment by Richard Martinet and the restoration of its Haussmannesque exterior. Situated in Paris's golden triangle, the Trémoille was built in 1883 as a private residence and became part of Forte in 1968. Before its recent purchase and redevelopment by the Scotsman Hotel Group, it was a Louis XV-style, tapestry-laden tribute to old France. While it retains its original grandeur, contemporary furniture and facilities were added to prepare it for the new century. In a separate development within the Trémoille, Conran & Partners were brought in to create the new Senso bar and restaurant. These would reflect the hotel's location in the supremely plush eighth arrondissement, and also establish it within the growing, cool and edgy Parisian music scene led by Hôtel Costes. The Trémoille had been a focal point of the city's jazz scene in the 1960s and the redevelopment was an opportunity to reawaken its musical heritage.

While the restaurant is ornate, the Senso bar has a Minimalist feel that just avoids being icy through the warmth of the dark-grey walls, the use of Venetian mirrors and a surprising dash of red. The long, pristine and pared-down space has the now seemingly obligatory limestone floor. Most of the furniture consists of cubic, ivory leather armchairs, with some rectangular sofas in the same material. The steel frames of the ivory-coloured tables are matched by the bar stools, which stand in front of a sheer, plain counter and the reflective panels of the display of glasses and bottles. The lighting above the bar alters the mood of the space, changing from blue during the day to red at night – when Senso really gets into its stride, with the house DJ, Pascal Lamy, providing lounge music on most nights. The bar continues to be a tremendous draw for the fashionistas, lounge lizards and media types who are the lifeblood of the designer-bar scene. The Trémoille has always been celebrity laden, but Senso has enabled it to become more widely fashionable.

Red is used to give the bar a sexy edge. The entrance is a glowing red door, while illuminated red glass separates the main space from a more private seating area where the ivory theme is replaced by red and grey banquettes. Damask cushions provide a sensual, elegant touch that links the bar with the more exuberant design of the rest of the hotel, including the Senso restaurant. This consists of three panelled rooms which share the grey and ivory theme of the bar, but the furniture frames and flooring are dark timber, while the curtains are silk. Custom-made Murano chandeliers add a touch of contemporary elegance, along with two large Expressionist paintings.

Left: La Trémoille, Paris.
Designed by Conran & Partners, the Senso bar and restaurant have opened the historical hotel up to a new breed of design-savvy movers and shakers

Opposite: La Trémoille, Paris. The Senso bar has an elegant, contemporary Minimalism. The blue light-panel in the ceiling above the bar counter changes to red as the evening gets under way, creating a moodier music lounge

Bar	Senso
Hotel	Hôtel de la Trémoille
Address	16 rue de la Trémoille, 75008 Paris, France
Telephone	+33 (0)1 56 52 14 14
Opening hours	Mon, Sun 11am–11pm, Tues–Sat 11am–2am
Number of seats	100
Design style	Cool, Minimalist chic hiding a warm heart
Clientele	The hotel has traditionally been associated with a vast array of celebrities, from Orson Welles to Johnny Depp. The regular Senso bar crowd are fashionistas, creatives and lounge lizards
Speciality drinks/cocktails	Imaginative list of own cocktails
Music	Lounge/jazz, with DJ Wed–Sun
Membership details/ door policy	None

Above: **La Trémoille, Paris.** Senso's principal theme of ivory leather furniture and grey walls is lifted by illuminated red glass panels

Left: **La Trémoille, Paris.** The limestone flooring in the bar turns upwards before giving way to the simple, sharp counter

Above: **La Trémoille, Paris.** In the more private area to the side of the main bar, red and grey leather banquettes provide an intimate, sexier ambience

Right: **La Trémoille, Paris.** Although the Senso restaurant is thematically linked to the bar through its colour scheme, it has a more traditional sense of style, with panelled walls, silk curtains and Murano chandeliers

Long Bar, Raffles

Architects 61

Location: Singapore
Completion date: 1921 (restored 1991)

The Long Bar is one of the most famous bars in the world, but only found its current home on Level 2 of the Raffles Hotel Arcade in 1991 during Architects 61's substantial renovation and restoration of the hotel. It has an itinerant history, starting at the beginning of the 20th century when it was the informal Rendezvous of Planters on Cad's Alley. Plantation owners who were staying at Raffles on a weekend break from Malaya used to line up their tables so that they had a good vantage point from which to study passing womenfolk on the Bras Basah Road. The bar takes its current name from its relocation to the hotel's Old Ballroom in 1921, when it was fitted with a 12-metre (40-foot) bar counter that ran the width of the room. It was moved to the other side of the ballroom in the early 1980s before settling into its new home a decade later. Raffles itself is named after Singapore's founder, Sir Stamford Raffles, and started life in 1887 as a 10-room bungalow on the site it occupies today.

It's hard to tell from the interior that its latest incarnation dates from 1991. The bar resolutely takes its stylistic inspiration from its original clientele. With its mass of large-leafed plant life sprouting among rattan and cane furniture, and paddle fans on the ceiling, it evokes a 1920s plantation that is just about holding back the jungle. The floors are tiled and graced with oriental carpets, while the timber spiral staircase to the second level leads to more cane and rattan seating, with the added sophistication of teak loungers. However, it is perhaps the veranda, which wraps around the long wooden bar on the first level, that is the most favoured spot for a Singapore sling. Invented by Ngiam Tong Boon before the bar's name changed in 1921, this is among the world's most famous cocktails and having one at the Long Bar has become a touristic rite of passage. Sipping a sling while throwing peanut shells on the floor may seem a little corny; and the Long Bar is a world away from the bustling, ardently modern city that Singapore has become. This doesn't diminish the pleasure of the experience – after all, it is part of a tradition that has been thoughtfully and authentically preserved.

Raffles is meant to offer a taste of the old world, and this is borne out by the similarly traditional style of some of its other bars, including the Writers Bar and the Bar and Billiards Room. With its mix of Eastern and European sophistication creating the atmosphere of a colonial club, the latter may seem tame now, but the last tiger to be killed in Singapore was prowling under its formerly elevated floor when it was shot in 1902.

Opposite: **Raffles, Singapore.** The main lobby of the hotel

Left: **Raffles, Singapore.** Raffles developed from a 10-room single-storey building in 1887 to become one of the world's best-known luxury hotels, with 103 suites and 18 restaurants and bars

Bar	The Long Bar
Hotel	Raffles
Address	No 1 Beach Road, Singapore 189673
Telephone	+65 6412 1229
Opening hours	Mon–Thur, Sun 11am–12.30am, Fri–Sat 11am–1.30am
Number of seats	292
Design style	1920s Malayan plantation
Clientele	Mostly tourists, some locals
Speciality drinks/ cocktails	The Singapore Sling, which includes gin, cherry brandy and Cointreau, started life here in around 1915. Other favourites are the Million Dollar Cocktail and the Tiger Lily
Music	Live show band playing a mixture of music, but don't expect acid jazz
Membership details/ door policy	None

Above: **Raffles, Singapore.** The Long Bar is decked out with rattan and cane furniture and evokes the style of a 1920s Malayan plantation

Below: **Raffles, Singapore.** The Bar and Billiards Room features the main bar, Cigar Divan, Martini Bar, garden terrace and Billiard Room. Like the Long Bar, rattan features heavily, but it also houses surprises like Miguel Carcio Martins's red Murano- and passementarie-inspired chandeliers

Above: **Raffles, Singapore.** With its heavy, dark wood furniture the Writers Bar is more European in flavour than the other bars, but no less traditional. It pays homage to writers such as Noel Coward and Rudyard Kipling who either stayed at Raffles or wrote about it. Joseph Conrad is thought to have been one the hotel's earliest guests

Commonwealth Club

MoreySmith

Location: London
Completion date: 1998

The Commonwealth Club was founded in 1868 in a building on London's Northumberland Avenue and was typical of most gentlemen's clubs in Victorian England. The Commonwealth, whose formal head is the monarch, is a voluntary association of states that were once part of the British Empire. The Royal Commonwealth Society (RCS), which runs the club, was established for those involved in the relationship between Britain and its colonies.

Historically, it has been impossible to disentangle the concept of the Commonwealth from that of empire. While other Victorian clubs were able to continue blithely, without altering so much as a fireplace, the Commonwealth Club was badly damaged by its association with a past that many would prefer to forget. The building was overhauled by Sir Herbert Baker in 1935, and numerous stuffed animal-heads were removed, but he added touches that would confound modern thinking – such as studding the Portland stone exterior with empire medallions, and adding an empire clock to show that 'the sun never sets' on the British Empire. By the beginning of the 1990s membership and use of the club were dwindling, and the RCS was faced with a mostly empty building and the need to spend £5 million just on maintaining it.

The solution was brave and radical. The RCS wanted to show that its role in the modern era is about understanding, communication and multiculturalism, rather than power and abuse. It sold 80 per cent of the unwieldy premises to a hotel chain, and hired architects MoreySmith to use the remaining 20 per cent to reinvent the organisation in the eyes of the public. The result, completed in 1998, is exemplar of an architectural redefinition of functional perception.

The new journey begins outside. Panes of coloured glass in the exterior windows of the club introduce new motifs of transparency and colour. Baker's entranceway, adorned by sculpted figures holding up a first-floor balcony, is now the door to the hotel while, through the modest reception area, the door to the new club is clear, frameless glass. The darkness, formality and secrecy that typified Victorian club culture are banished as the large restaurant/bar area of the ground floor opens up. White walls, light cherry-wood floors and vibrant colours dominate the interior, which features a suspended, glass, dining-room pod. Red, green and blue semicircular banquettes are a distinctive element in the restaurant. Twisting ribbons of these colours, plus yellow, are used in the mosaic frontages of both the upstairs and downstairs bars. The ribbons also form the new logo of the RCS, designed by MoreySmith, which clearly expresses the society's desire to advocate the value of the cooperation between the nations of the Commonwealth, making a virtue of the link between disparate countries.

Some associations with the past remain, but they have been reinterpreted. Baker's clock is now suspended in midair and framed with transparent glass, while the walnut panelling is reused in the members' lounges in the basement. This floor is very flexible and has become a key source of income for the RCS through its use for functions and conferences. There is an ironic twist to the Commonwealth Club's redefinition and the reduction in its space: so many outside organisations want to hire the facilities that the club now needs to expand into the building next door. MoreySmith will again lead the development.

Opposite: **Commonwealth Club, London.** The pod-like, glass dining room, which is often used for meetings, is suspended above the ground floor restaurant and bar. Access to it is along a glass walkway from the small mezzanine bar

Club	Commonwealth Club
Address	18 Northumberland Avenue, London WC2N 5BJ, UK
Telephone	+44 (0)20 7930 6733
Opening hours	Mon–Sat 7am–midnight
Design style	Colourful and contemporary
Clientele	Surprisingly young, global blend of diplomatic workers and businesspeople
Speciality drinks/cocktails	The usual
Music	Nothing undiplomatic
Membership details/ door policy	Members only (£50–£210 pa, depending on age and residence, with £25–£100 registration fee)

Above: **Commonwealth Club, London.** Elements of the old club have been reused but reinterpreted. Sir Herbert Baker's 1935 empire clock, designed to show how the sun never set on Britain's vast empire, is now set in transparent glass and suspended on steel rods

Below: **Commonwealth Club, London.** The coloured chairs in the restaurant reflect the RCS's new identity. The bar, on the ground floor, is fronted by red-topped stools under a canopy created by the mezzanine walkway. The upstairs bar has circular, pod-like chairs covered in the colours of the new logo

Above: **Commonwealth Club, London.** The subterranean members' lounges feature traditional furniture and muted colours. The walnut panelling is from the former club, which was famed for using woods from all over the Commonwealth

Left: **Commonwealth Club, London.** The bar on the mezzanine is directly above the ground-level bar. Both frontages feature mosaics of the RCS's new logo, designed by MoreySmith, which emphasises the society's modern, vibrant role in supporting multinational cooperation

Above: **Commonwealth Club, London.** The idea of a heavy, imposing doorway to the club was abandoned in favour of clear, frameless glass. The Mandarin stone floor of the reception gives way to the cherry wood of the restaurant. The red, curving banquette is designed by MoreySmith

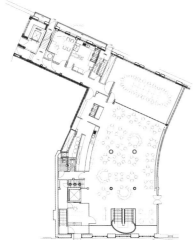

Above: **Commonwealth Club, London.** Plan of the ground floor, which is principally made up of the restaurant and bar with a function room to the rear

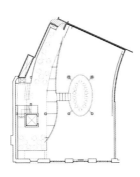

Above: **Commonwealth Club, London.** Seating around the upstairs bar and stairway to the mezzanine level leads across glass flooring to the suspended dining room

Reform Club

Sir Charles Barry

Location: London
Completion date: 1841

When members of the Reform Club talk about significant changes to its décor, they are probably referring to the work done in 1878 by Edward Middleton Barry, son of the original architect, Sir Charles Barry, or to the fact that someone has repositioned a favourite chair. During the revolution that has occurred in club and hotel design, the Reform Club, like many of its Victorian siblings, has remained unchanged.

The original design of the building, in 1841, incorporated revolutionary aspects that reflected the club's *raison d'être* – it was set up by progressive politicians and other members of society who wanted to extend the franchise, granted to prosperous middle-class men in the 1832 Reform Act, to a greater number of male voters. No particular element was innovative in itself but Barry used an unusual combination of newish or rarely used techniques, including an air-ventilation system and gas lighting. His first major commission had been the Travellers' Club, the Reform Club's neighbour on Pall Mall. Rather than being yet another icon of the Greek classical revival that continued to hold sway over major British architects, this had drawn on the palazzos of the Italian Renaissance. The interior of the Reform Club, behind its solid Portland stone facade, was a step further. Barry took the design of the Palazzo Farnese and acclimatised it to the British weather and character.

Even though the Reform Club had its origins in the extension of the franchise it is still physically aloof. The entrance is withdrawn from the street, up some steps, and is immediately followed by a protective, inhospitable lobby – a buffer zone to stop unwanted guests and the hoi polloi entering. However, immediately through the next door is the building's architectural showpiece: the saloon. This is a grand, beautifully proportioned courtyard, 18 metres (60 feet) high, surrounded by the club's two principal floors. It is topped by a domed skylight, part of which is made up of lozenge-shaped panes set in a cast-iron grid, foreshadowing Sir Norman Foster's acclaimed Great Court roof at the British Museum. Surprisingly, Barry's faith in the British weather was such that he originally wanted to leave the courtyard exposed to the elements.

Any idea of democracy did not extend to the layout of the club. This is a secret world where the entrances to the various club rooms – the Reform's real heart – are concealed in the saloon's corners. The main ones include the library, the drawing room, the morning room and the smoking room. Some rooms were swapped around during various, early refurbishments – the library became the smoking room while the drawing room became the library – but in general the look of the club has remained remarkably unaltered. Some of the original Taprell and Holland furnishings are still there, while replacements consciously maintain the house style.

Although Victorian clubs like the Reform were a response to the emergence of the new, professional middle classes, the look is stately, even more so than in the original, aristocratic clubs of the Regency period. The ceilings are high and the rooms are long and column-bedecked, while the colours never vary from the traditional red, green, brown and gold palette that is expected in a gentlemen's club. Expectation – the certainty that the Reform Club will remain unaltered while the world changes rapidly and inexplicably – is the key to its continuation. It is far less likely to have a design overhaul now than it was in 1878.

Opposite: **Reform Club, London**. The columns in the saloon are made of stone finished with sienna scagiola. Elsewhere in the club they are scagiola or real marble

Club	Reform Club
Address	104 Pall Mall, London SW1Y 5EW, UK
Telephone	+44 (0)20 7930 9374
Opening hours	Main bar 11am–3pm, 6pm–9pm; upstairs bar 11am–11pm
Number of seats	Members can drink in various club rooms
Design style	Neoclassical meets Italian palazzo
Clientele	Usually politicians with liberal leanings, but Tina Turner had a recent birthday party here
Speciality drinks/cocktails	None, but a good range of whiskies
Music	No
Membership details/door policy	Members only

Right: Reform Club, London. The furniture in the smoking room includes button-leather armchairs. The Reform Club has so many books that the library is not big enough to contain all of them

Below: Reform Club, London. The Reform Club, seen here in an engraving of a picture by Moore, joined the grand line of club buildings along Pall Mall in 1841

Above: Reform Club, London. George Moore's impression of the corridor of the saloon, soon after the club opened. The space was used for a sword-fighting scene in the James Bond film *Die Another Day*

Right: Reform Club, London. Meals are served in this long gallery. It has a coffered ceiling and feels lighter and more airy than the club's other rooms

Left and above: **Reform Club, London.** The ornate library, which was formerly the drawing room, is decorated throughout in green and gold. Many new clubs have borrowed the idea of buttoned leather chesterfields from their Victorian counterparts

Below: **Reform Club, London.** The club may have been born out of concepts of liberal democracy but its entranceway is aloof and forbidding, a characteristic shared by many Victorian clubs

Claridge's Bar, Claridge's

David Collins

Location: London
Completion date: 1998

When Claridge's opened its new bar in September 1998, David Collins's award-laden design added a new chapter to the significant history of its drinking establishments. The hotel, which is now a Grade II-listed building, effectively dates from 1854 when the original small Claridge's merged with the larger Mivart's hotel. It was rebuilt in 1898 with a new bar that was separate from the other public rooms. This featured 'American drinks', as cocktails were then known in Britain, under the stewardship of barmaid Ada Coleman – reportedly the first woman in the country to devise a cocktail. Claridge's was refurbished in an ardently contemporary Art Deco-style by Basil Ionides in the 1920s, with further additions by Oswald Milne in 1930.

Collins chose to enhance the bar's Art Deco features, giving them a contemporary twist in a design where attention to detail is very evident. The result is a seamless combination of new and old that marks Claridge's Bar out as an impressive example of a classic establishment that has embraced contemporary design without forfeiting its sense of grandeur and traditional luxury.

The white, curving, marble-topped bar counter is the centrepiece of the small space. The large number of tall and sturdy, burgundy leather bar stools immediately suggests that the bar is meant to be intimate and convivial. A combination of mirrored panels behind the counter and light-bulbs along the sides and bottom of its frontage helps to evoke the old-world glamour of a stage dressing room. Sage-coloured walls and wood flooring combine with burgundy for the armchairs and leather-covered banquettes to maintain warmth and intimacy below the high ceiling, which features intricate coving that steps up towards a central, green chandelier.

As well as the main area there is an intimate snuggery, with sage panelling on the low ceiling and the walls. Lighting is provided by a six-sided ceiling light and uplights on the walls. Both spaces feature small, round, polished wooden tables.

Claridge's Bar has an old-fashioned, very British sense of glamour; but it is hip and stylish enough to be a fitting backdrop for the dynamic movers and shakers of contemporary culture.

While Collins reinvented the bar, New York designer Thierry Despont was brought in to redesign Claridge's foyer, where he created a second, more formal space for everything from tea to cocktails. Inspired by photographs of the hotel's 1930s ballroom extension he, like Collins, evoked the Art Deco era, adding a contemporary twist with a Dale Chihuly chandelier. After Claridge's, Collins went on to design the Blue Bar at the Berkeley, Locanda Locatelli's restaurant and Kabaret's Prophecy, a new nightclub, all in London.

Opposite: Claridge's, London. Claridge's originally consisted of a row of individual houses. Richard D'Oyly Carte took it over in 1894 and promptly demolished them to make way for the current, purpose-built hotel

Bar	Claridge's Bar
Hotel	Claridge's
Address	Davies Street, Mayfair, London W1A 2JQ, UK
Telephone	+44 (0)20 7629 8860
Opening hours	Mon–Sat noon–1am, Sun 4pm–midnight
Number of seats	45
Design style	Art Deco with a contemporary twist
Clientele	Grown-up media luvvies who like style but aren't going out of their way to make a statement
Speciality drinks/cocktails	The gin-based Mayfair Classic and the Flapper, a frothy champagne cocktail. Features a vintage-champagne library
Music	It may waft in gently from the lobby
Membership details/ door policy	None

Above: **Claridge's, London.** Claridge's Bar includes Art Deco features like the white marble bar-top that echo the hotel's 1920s refurbishment. The thin legs of the top-heavy, burgundy-covered bar stools are surprisingly sturdy. The centrepiece of the high, coved ceiling is a green glass chandelier which adds a sybaritic but contemporary touch

Left: **Claridge's, London.** The snuggery, to the rear of the main bar, is an intimate, sage-panelled room which also features burgundy leather banquettes and poufs

Above: **Claridge's, London.** The hotel has a second place in which to enjoy a cocktail. Thierry Despont's new foyer is inspired by photographs of the hotel's 1930s ballroom, but he has added contemporary elements like the Dale Chihuly chandelier

Right: **Claridge's, London.** Claridge's Bar has its own entrance from Davies Street which leads straight into the main bar

American Bar, The Savoy

Location: London
Completion date: 1973

Historically, the American Bar at the Savoy is one of London's most important hotel bars. Its current interior, which is around 30 years old, may look dated in comparison to the Long Bar, the Blue Bar and others that have led the hotel-bar revival in the city, but it remains immune to fashion. The oldest existing cocktail bar in London, it has an assured place in history and it continues to deliver exactly what its clientele expects.

Richard D'Oyly Carte opened the Savoy in 1889 but the bar was not established until 1898, following a refit of the hotel's public rooms, during the wave of enthusiasm for 'American drinks' that emerged towards the end of the 19th century. Since then, the bar has had a string of famous bartenders, including Ada Coleman, who came to it from Claridge's, and Harry Craddock, the inventor of the White Lady, whose *The Savoy Cocktail Book* was first published in 1930 and remains in print.

The American Bar was originally on the river side of the hotel before being moved to its current location in 1904, when two new blocks were added to the original building. It was at the forefront of the golden age of cocktails in the 1920s and 1930s – during which it sported its most contemporary décor. This was probably heavily influenced by D'Oyly Carte's granddaughter Dorothy, who took an interest in the interior design of the Savoy Group hotels. With its crisscrossed mirrors, angular furniture, geometrically patterned carpets and rugs, and suspended, stepped oblong light-fittings, the bar expressed the very latest in Art Deco. If its design had remained unaltered since then, its interior would still be considered one of the most stunning in London. However, its Art Deco style has been reinvented to suit the contemporary tastes of various periods.

By the early 1950s, a surprising amount of bamboo cane had been introduced along with pattern-printed curtains and a mottled ceiling. The current 1970s interior re-evokes the earlier style, especially through the consoles, whose design draws on preserved areas in the rest of the hotel, and in the style of the mirrors. However, the rounded cutout of the bar, the similarly rounded edges to the wall corners and fittings, and the busy patterns of the furnishings make the interior a child of its time. Some improvements have been made over the years: women are no longer consigned to a separate lounge.

The wealthy, conservative clientele enjoys the atmosphere, the impressive cocktails and the exemplary service, and is unlikely to want to exchange the American Bar's reserved, cruise-ship charm for the ironic assault of a Philippe Starck interior. If the bar does receive a design overhaul, perhaps it should revel in, rather than merely suggest, its golden age with a total return to Art Deco. This would ensure its immunity from passing trends for many years to come.

Opposite: **The Savoy, London.** The famous, metal-clad entranceway to the hotel continues to make a stylish, luxurious Art Deco statement to passers-by

Bar	American Bar
Hotel	The Savoy
Address	Strand, London WC2R 0EU, UK
Telephone	+44 (0)20 7836 4343
Opening hours	Mon–Fri 4pm–1am, Sat 2pm–1am
Number of seats	50
Design style	1970s translation of Art Deco
Clientele	Hotel guests, tourists, pre-theatre visitors, local businesspeople
Speciality drinks/cocktails	White Lady, Savoy Affair, Vanilla Caiperoska, champagne cocktails, classic martinis
Music	Pianist plays a selection of contemporary music from 7.30pm. Easy listening rather than trip-hop
Membership details/ door policy	Dress: smart casual. No membership policy

Above: The Savoy, London. By the 1930s the American Bar was the perfect arena for a combination of the cocktail's golden age and Art Deco style. The octagonal fireplace was set into a mirror-panelled wall while the oblong light-fittings, suspended from metal clasps, were the height of contemporary design

Right: The Savoy, London. By the 1950s a passion for bamboo and foliage was reflected in the design of the American Bar. Perhaps the designer had been to the Long Bar in Singapore

Left: The Savoy, London. The current interior of the American Bar bar dates from 1973, although there has been some refurbishment since then. Some features, like the mirrors, successfully evoke its Art Deco past; others, like the console between the windows, are drawn from historical interiors elsewhere in the hotel. The bar features a 'royal box', a private room within the space

Below: The Savoy, London. The bar counter has been at the end of the space since at least the early 1950s. The American Bar is decorated with images of people who have visited it, taken by the acclaimed celebrity photographer Terry O'Neill

next generation

The late 1990s revival of cocktail culture and the new enthusiasm for hotel bars and members' clubs have led to an impressive array of recent ventures across the world. There has been a particularly strong trend towards merging the exclusiveness of the private members' bar with the social facilities of the hotel. The success of the Met Bar in London awoke the hotel industry to a new possibility: rigorous exclusivity, combined with innovative design, could offer a kudos that was previously unimaginable in this sector. Worldwide, some of the most interesting and ground-breaking designs are for bars that willingly quote the Met Bar as an inspiration. In fact, Q! The Bar at the Q! Hotel in Berlin and the INK Club Bar in Singapore have made great leaps beyond the Met in terms of design.

The concepts developed by Ian Schrager and Philippe Starck may have reached their zenith at London's Sanderson, but they have also bred a new generation of hotel bars and clubs (apart from the fact that every new or refurbished establishment across the globe seems to refer to itself as a 'boutique hotel'). The designers of many of the bars in this chapter quote the Schrager/Starck concept of 'hotel as theatre' in some form or other. Their

Next Generation

designs are informed by a new understanding that the social spaces of hotels can provoke drama, offering unique experiences through unique design. Schrager reconceived luxury as being 'access to new experiences'; Karim Rashid, whose MyHotel Brighton opens in 2005, said the hotel is 'somewhere to have an experience you cannot have anywhere else … an individual moment'. It is now almost taken for granted that a new hotel must have a bar that delivers the unexpected. Little signposts of corporatism may be allowed to creep into elements of hotel-room design, but woe betide the designer whose bar doesn't incorporate several ironic jokes and a previously unimaginable feature involving ostrich leather.

The original stylish and innovatively designed hotels and clubs of the new wave were confined to cities that have long been at the forefront of advances in culture. New York, London, Berlin and Melbourne are all sophisticated but daring focal points for cultural endeavour, and have a reputation for making a splash beyond their countries' borders. More recent design innovations are broader based and are born out of specific environments: the designers may talk an international, conceptual language, but their grand physical statements are reactions to local developments. The Roppongi Hills Club, sitting atop a huge tower, draws the eye towards a very Japanese cultural redevelopment in an area of Tokyo. Bilbao's major new hotels take their inspiration from the nearby Guggenheim Museum, while in Singapore the

Fullerton and the INK Club Bar are linked to the city's ongoing reinvention of itself as a wealthy, cosmopolitan centre for innovative contemporary architecture and design. Even Eva Jiricna's new Hotel Josef in stately old Prague is a very conscious statement about the innovation of the Czech modernism that predated the Soviet era.

The success of the new breed of hotel bars and members' clubs is indelibly linked to the public's dissatisfaction with the corporate homogeneity of the architectural landscape. It is no coincidence that these successful designs find their root in the particular rather than the transglobal.

Below: **Roppongi Hills Club, Tokyo.** This private members' club, in the redeveloped cultural quarter of Roppongi, overlooks Tokyo. It has a vast array of separate facilities for personal and business entertainment. Pictured is a private dining room in the Hiyakumi-an Japanese restaurant

Long Bar, Sanderson

Philippe Starck

Location: London
Completion date: 2000

Within six months of the opening of the St Martin's Lane in London, Ian Schrager and Philippe Starck teamed up for another new hotel with another startling concept, just a mile away. After the resounding success of the Light Bar there a great deal was expected the new venture's bar. The Long Bar more than lived up to expectations and remains one of the capital's favourite cocktail destinations.

The Sanderson, which was converted from a 1958 building created for the Sanderson fabric company, was conceived of as an 'urban spa' (930 square metres/10,000 square feet is given over to spa facilities) that would provide an antidote to the fast but homogenous city. In design terms, it is perhaps the culmination of the Schrager/Starck reinvention of the hotel. Extravagant, signature gestures are mediated by the classiness and elegance of the spa style. Humour and wit are still very evident, but the Sanderson has a pared-down sense of balance and depth that goes beyond their exuberance. This refined luxury, which should not be confused with Minimalism, is nowhere more evident than in the Long Bar.

The huge lobby of the hotel is multifaceted and includes indoor and outdoor spaces. The large, open reception area features Salvador Dali's red-lips sofa, Tom Sachs' *Chanel Chainsaw* sculpture and a front desk of acid-etched glass that houses five screens displaying video art. To the right lies the Long Bar, sandwiched between the glass facade of the building and the open-air courtyard. From outside the hotel the bar glows with mystery – the glazing is dressed in sheer gauze curtains that allow only a hint of what lies beyond. Consequently, even though it is in the lobbythe bar has has an air of privacy and protection from the outside world. Hanging against the gauze is a traditional portrait of a British bulldog with a black eye. Starck has left a calling card – while British tradition looks on, a Frenchman has reinvented the concept of luxury.

The bar counter dominates the slim space. An elongated, onyx rectangle, 24 metres (80 feet) long, it incorporates lights so that it glows from within. The stainless-steel bar top overhangs the counter, providing room for the bar stools. These are a major feature of the design and convey a message to the Long Bar's clientele. Set on silver-leaf frames, the white upholstered backs carry photographer Ramak Fazel's image of a large, single eye: bargoers are here to see and be seen, and the designer has got their number.

Those who do not wish to play the preening game head to the more exclusive Purple Bar off the main lobby. With its miniature Queen Anne chairs, Venetian glass and dark-purple wall coverings, it looks as if Alice in Wonderland has opened a tiny 1970s nightclub. Both it and the Long Bar are hugely popular with the rich and famous.

If the Sanderson has one failing, it is that more is not made of one of the glories of the original building: a beautiful stained-glass window by John Piper. It is in the Billiard Room, but is not often seen other than by people attending functions or meetings.

Bar	Long Bar
Hotel	Sanderson
Address	50 Berners Street, London W1T 3NG, UK
Telephone	+44 (0)20 7300 1400
Opening hours	Mon–Sat 10am–1am, Sun 10am–midnight
Number of seats	50
Design style	Glowing white rectangle with one eye on the celebrities
Clientele	It's the heart of film and media land and also popular with pop princesses such as Kylie, but there's also a wannabe element, which is excluded from the hotel's Purple Bar
Speciality drinks/cocktails	Martinis including the Sanderson, the Elderflower and the Lychee
Music	DJs Wed–Fri
Membership details/door policy	It's a public bar, but its popularity means doormen can get selective

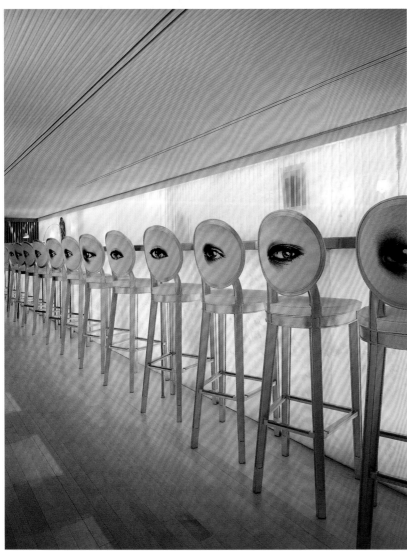

Left: Sanderson, London. Detail of the white upholstered Long Bar stools. Ramack Fazel's image of a female eye overlooks proceedings, playing with the customers' desire to see and be seen

Right: Sanderson, London. The tiny, dark, Purple Bar admits only hotel residents and their guests. Miniature chairs and tiny tables stand before the huge granite bar

Below: Sanderson, London. The 24 metre (80-foot) onyx counter glows along the length of the Long Bar. There is no raised display of bottles and glasses so the space remains linear

Above: Sanderson, London. One of the delights of
the hotel is the Garden Courtyard, which can be
reached from the Long Bar. Inspired by Japanese
gardens, it still features aspects of Philip Hick's
original, late 1950s design

Left: Sanderson, London. The extensive Agua Spa features an eclectic mix of furniture including 18th-century Italian chairs, stainless-steel tables and Venetian mirrors. It offers a full range of treatments and a gymnasium

Below: Sanderson, London. The Penthouse and Apartment suites, adorned with rugs inspired by Filippino Lippi, have no interior walls

Q! The Bar, Q!

GRAFT

Location: Berlin
Completion date: 2004

The emergence of Q! on the west side of Berlin is further evidence that the east is no longer the sole preserve of radical design. Its name comes from Ku'Damm, which is itself short for Kurfürstendamm, a street and surrounding area that is rapidly asserting itself as a mini style-capital.

The design of the hotel is based on a fluid approach to structure and the use of natural materials. The centrepiece is Q! The Bar, which acknowledges London's Met Bar as an inspiration to the extent that it is available only for hotel guests and members; and the Met's Ben Reed is bar consultant. However, comparisons with the London establishment stop there. In design terms Q! is a leap forward: the use of folds, creases and waves to create multilevel zones and furniture is unique.

The bar itself slices through the space, allowing for a distinct restaurant/bar to the rear and the main bar in front. It is this frontal area that seems to be the culmination of GRAFT architect Thomas Willemeit's desire to create a cocoon-like feeling throughout the hotel. It is a seamless, warm and enclosed environment that establishes its own parameters – Willemeit was keen that the bar should be an enveloping stage set, within which guests' personal, lifestyle dramas would be played out.

The red flooring of the main area sweeps upwards to create new levels and curves sharply to form sloping walls, while establishing inbuilt seating on its journey. This inner skin also folds over to make the ceiling of the bar area. Illuminated white panels are inserted into the angles where the waves break away from the main plane, while the frontage of the bar counter is a larger panel of white, which provides the most obvious light source in the space. As well as the moulded benches created by the folds of red there are low, geometrical divans, covered with suede, that mirror the angles of the flooring.

The exclusivity of Q! The Bar is reinforced by both the structural architecture and the interior design. There is a second, private entrance to the bar along a corridor that comes out at the courtyard, so members do not have to enter the hotel, and the staff wear designer uniforms by Strellson and St.Emile. By day, the bar's glass frontage is veiled by a semitransparent curtain that partially obscures the interior from curious passers-by. At night, as a result of careful uplighting by floor lamps, this becomes an impenetrable wall. Gauze curtains are used throughout the interior to create private zones for the especially media-shy.

Q! The Bar is specifically designed for 'artists and creatives, for individualists, lifestyle experts, opinion leaders, multipliers …' Presumably, the last will be pleased to find that the bedrooms, with their natural colours and textures of slate and wood, are also beautifully designed.

GRAFT's most prestigious work before Q! was a studio and guesthouse for Brad Pitt in Los Angeles, but its diverse work in the fields of car design, art installations and music-video sets reflects a leaning towards the conceptual fluidity and hybridization that has been borne out in the hotel. Q! is owned by the private Loock-Hotels Group, which also runs the Alexander Plaza in Berlin and is currently rolling out an expansion programme throughout Germany.

Opposite: **Q!, Berlin.** The hotel's facade may not be particularly adventurous but the reception area introduces the unique design of Q! The Bar, which takes up much of the ground floor. The reception desk rises out of the flooring like a wave while the wall slopes inwards and arcs over to form the ceiling

Bar	Q! The Bar
Hotel	Q!
Address	Knesebeckstrasse 67, 10623 Berlin, Germany
Telephone	+49 (0)30 810066 0
Opening hours	Mon–Sat 6pm–3am, Sun 6pm–midnight
Number of seats	75–85
Design style	Ultramodern red cocoon that could double as an interior skateboard park
Clientele	Artistic, media and celebrity crowds playing away from their usual haunts in east Berlin
Speciality drinks/cocktails	Q! cocktail, specially created by the Met Bar's Ben Reed
Music	Lounge
Membership details/door policy	Members and hotel guests only

Left: **Q!, Berlin.** The red flooring rises up in waves to create different levels and zones in the front area of the bar. The angles formed as the waves break away from the main plane are used for lighting

Below: **Q!, Berlin.** Privacy and mystery are created by the gauze curtains across the hotel's front window. Semitransparent by day, uplighting makes them impermeable at night. The warm feeling of GRAFT's cocoon is reinforced by the fire in the front area's dark, almost Cubist central feature

Opposite: **Q!, Berlin.** One section of the red flooring folds upwards to create inbuilt seating while another curves over to enclose the bar area. The bar counter, which divides the front space from the restaurant area, is fronted by an illuminated white panel, and softer, more discreet light comes from the angle between the wall and ceiling

Above: **Q!, Berlin.** The rear section of the space is multifunctional. During the course of the day it is used as the guests' breakfast room, as the restaurant and as additional bar space. The booths on the left can be veiled by the gauze curtains, giving members an even greater sense of privacy and exclusivity

Above: **Q!, Berlin.** One of the hotel's most unusual features is the Wellness Sandroom. Hot sand floors, heated loungers and aromatherapy oils create an atmosphere of calm

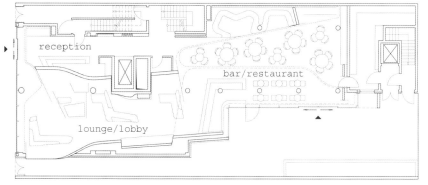

reception

bar/restaurant

lounge/lobby

Right: **Q!, Berlin.** Members can access Q! The Bar without entering the hotel by using the corridor that runs along the bottom of the ground-floor plan

UNA Lounge, UNA Hotel Vittoria

Fabio Novembre

Location: Florence
Completion date: 2003

With both feet placed firmly in the past Florence is not, perhaps, the most likely place to find cutting-edge hotel design. However, Michele Bönan's conceptual Gallery Hotel Art, which was something of a sensation when it opened in the city in 1999, has been joined by UNA Hotel Vittoria. The owners of the new UNA Hotel chain wanted to attract tourists to a relatively unknown area of Florence and, wishing to make a dramatic statement, turned to Fabio Novembre. The young Italian, whose L'Atlantique restaurant and Divina nightclub in Milan brought him to the forefront of design, has said that he believes he is among 'the last defenders of the third dimension'. He is nothing if not dramatic.

The conservative exterior of the listed building, set in a small courtyard, does little to disturb the historical environment; but it hides an interior that is the realisation of a radical, passionate dream that is designed to be specific to Florence. Novembre dislikes the idea of design-hotels that embody some form of reductive, international aesthetic and wanted to create a unique prelude to the city. In his typically bold design statement he says: 'I envision the hotel as a tree, whose far-reaching branches extend across the world, but with roots firmly embedded in its native soil.' At its heart the design is about contact, in both social and historical terms.

The hotel lobby, which also acts as the bar, immediately reveals the radical core of Novembre's vision. Floor to ceiling is wrapped in a spiral of typically Florentine floral mosaic that curves up from the floor to form the reception desk. To the left the spiral is mirrored by the seating in the UNA Lounge, which consists of two black-and-red coils. Designed by Novembre and manufactured by Tino Sana, these embrace people who sit on them while placing them in immediate contact with other guests. The sofa-spirals are accompanied by small square tables made up of the word 'LOVE'. It is as if Novembre is asking sitters to be seduced by Florence and by his design, while themselves playing the role of seducer. The bar counter is a simple box, graced by black-topped, silver stools.

The theme of contact is also prevalent in the restaurant, which features a reinvention of the communal table: a great curving, wooden 'S' snakes around the pillars, curving diners in towards each other and thereby enhancing the possibility of interaction. Above, lighting comes through stained glass that follows the curve of the table and serves once again to marry Florentine history with contemporary design. Lest anyone should think that Novembre has saved the drama solely for the showy, public areas of the hotel, he has brought memories of the Uffizi gallery into the corridors, where doors are faux historical portraits set in golden frames.

The UNA Hotel chain continues its expansion, with individual hotels that reflect the particularities of their location. The latest, in Bologna, is by Marco Piva and is designed to reflect the city's place at a geographical and cultural crossroads.

Opposite: **UNA Hotel Vittoria, Florence.** A Florentine floral mosaic, manufactured by Bisazza, spirals from the entrance to form the reception desk

Bar	UNA Lounge
Hotel	UNA Hotel Vittoria
Address	Via Pisana 59, 50143 Florence, Italy
Telephone	+39 055 22771
Opening hours	10.30am–1am
Number of seats	20. The internal courtyard is also used in summer
Design style	Florentine history warped into a spiral wonderland
Clientele	Locals from the increasingly trendy Florence bar scene, and hotel guests
Speciality drinks/cocktails	The classics
Music	Hip hop and pop
Membership details/door policy	None

Above: **UNA Hotel Vittoria, Florence.** At the end of the lobby bar two black and red coils form intimate seating

Opposite: **UNA Hotel Vittoria, Florence.** The bar counter is plain and minimal so that it does not detract from the coiled heart of the bar area

Above: **UNA Hotel Vittoria, Florence.** The table tops sit on the square 'LOVE' tables manufactured by Tino Sana

Below: **UNA Hotel Vittoria, Florence.** The restaurant follows Fabio Novembre's wish to create social and historical 'contact'. The 'S' shape communal table, mirrored above by stained glass, almost forces strangers to interact

Above, left: **UNA Hotel Vittoria, Florence.** The doors to the hotel rooms are paintings in golden frames, which may be an unwelcome flashback for those who have been lost in the Uffizi all day

Left: **UNA Hotel Vittoria, Florence.** The exterior of the building, which is in a small courtyard, is listed and contrasts sharply with Novembre's interior

Above: UNA Hotel Vittoria, Florence.
The hotel's internal courtyard

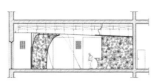

UNA Hotel Vittoria, Florence.
Section of the lobby/bar area

UNA Hotel Vittoria, Florence. Plan of
the lobby/bar area

West Bar, Sketch

Mourad Mazouz/Noé Douchaufour-Lawrance

Location: London
Completion date: 2002

There was a great deal of knowledgeable interest when Mourad Mazouz and chef Pierre Gagnaire decided to open a new venture in the disused former headquarters of the Royal Institute of British Architects. Mazouz, owner of the successful North African restaurant Momo, decided not to duck his head under the parapet and converted the 1779 town house into an extravagant, eclectic bar/restaurant/gallery complex. He worked with the French sculptor and interior designer Noé Duchaufour-Lawrance on the overall interior concept for the Grade II listed building, and commissioned further elements from an array of celebrated designers including Ron Arad, Jurgen Bey and architect Gabhan O'Keeffe.

The West Bar is accessible to the public by day, but from 5pm it is strictly a members-only area, available to Friends of Sketch. Conceived by Duchaufour-Lawrance and Mazouz as a blend of contemporary and 1960s styles, it features Eero Saarinen's vintage white Tulip chairs, adorned with cushions covered in a variety of black fabrics, along with black, tub chairs. The white flooring sweeps up to form the frontage of the bar counter while the shelving of the bar display marries the white of this lower level with the red of the walls. Contemporary details include eight moving, reflection sculptures by Vincent Leroy, Yoo Hee Ahn's installation of Swarovski crystal and Chris Levine's laser lighting. However, the sense of the original building has not been lost – the space is housed under the timber grid of its ceiling and dado rails still embellish the walls.

The West Bar is just one of the curiosities of Sketch, which is an explosion of forms, styles, influences and images rather than a subdued aesthetic melting pot. Even the entrance hall provides a disconcerting shock as Jurgen Bey's chairs are forced into it through an elastic skin. The restaurant spaces of the Lecture Room and Library, designed by O'Keeffe, also offer a twist on traditional opulence. The padded leather walls of the Library are studded with mirrors, while oversized urns stand before alcoves painted to look like dazzling

sunbursts. White tablecloths and miniature, Art Nouveau-style trees dress the tables, which are surrounded by stuffed, velvet-covered dining chairs. The pink-neon East Bar, for Friends of Sketch and diners only, is inspired by ovoid forms that prefigure the individual, enclosed, egg-like toilet pods – perhaps the most talked about feature of Sketch – in its all-white, unisex rest room.

By day, the Gallery is an art space where the public can sit on low leatherette-covered banquettes to watch conjoined video screens. At night, the banquettes give way to formal white dining chairs and figure-of-eight tables as it becomes a brasserie-restaurant.

The creation of Sketch reportedly cost over £10 million. This must go down as a huge gamble on a new kind of multifaceted venture where the distinctions between entertainment, art and interior design have become blurred. Except for mutterings about exorbitant food prices, it is a huge success, packed with a creative, elite crowd who are unlikely to wince at the bill and enjoy its radical onslaught on their senses. It's not short of Friends.

Opposite: Sketch, London. Black and white dominate the lower level of the West Bar's colour scheme. Saarinen's white Tulip chairs add a retro feel

Below: Sketch, London. A traditional ceiling and contemporary lighting displays create aesthetic contrasts in the West Bar, which is for the sole use of Friends of Sketch after 5pm

Bar	West Bar
Club	Sketch
Address	9 Conduit Street, London W1S 2XG, UK
Telephone	+44 (0) 870 777 4488
Opening hours	Mon–Sat noon–5pm (light lunches and drinks);
	Mon–Sat 5pm–2am (Friends of Sketch only)
Number of seats	30
Design style	1960s chic immersed in a 21st-century light show
Clientele	It still remains sharply hip, particularly with celebrity music makers
	and those who wish to make music with them. Robbie Williams,
	Justin Timberlake … The list is endless
Speciality drinks/cocktails	Martinis and champagne cocktails
Music	Varies, but often the very latest dance cuts
Membership details/door policy	Only Friends of Sketch in the evenings (£400 pa for the first year,
	then £300 pa)

Left: Sketch, London. The white flooring of the West Bar rises steeply to form the frontage of the bar counter. The top layer of the bar display introduces the red tones of the upper reaches of the room

Above: Sketch, London. The Lecture Room and Library restaurant features leather-clad, studded walls, gold leaf and stuffed velvet chairs. Reviewers were stunned not only by the décor but also by the prices, which led to the introduction of more affordable dishes

Below: Sketch, London. The interior of the East Bar is egg-shaped and houses a circular bar

Above: Sketch, London. The East Bar's unisex toilets feature individual, ovoid pods which were seen as a startling design innovation when Sketch opened in December 2002

Left: Sketch, London. The entrance features Jurgen Bey's chair-sculpture: grand chairs pushed through an elastic skin

Opposite and above: **Sketch, London.** By day, the all-white Gallery is open to members of the public, who can recline on banquettes while watching video art. At night, it becomes a brasserie-restaurant

Right: **Sketch, London.** Chocolate-coloured resin dribbles its way down the staircase, ensuring that customers realise Sketch is founded on a combined love of food and art

INK Club Bar, Raffles
The Plaza

Hirsch Bedner Associates

Location: Singapore
Completion date: 2004

The INK Club Bar is a recent addition to Raffles The Plaza in Singapore. Unlike the original Raffles, which glories in the city's history, the Plaza is associated with Singapore's new-found role as an international playground for contemporary architecture and design. The hotel, which features 769 rooms and suites with a choice of 17 restaurants and bars, is a high-rise that forms two connected towers with Swisshotel The Stamford.

The INK Club Bar is at the highly designed, exclusive end of the market and is one of a crop of new bars that are increasingly putting Singapore on the international entertainment scene. It models itself on the Met Bar in London in terms of exclusivity but, like Q! The Bar in Berlin, it leaves its exemplar behind in terms of interior design. Curiously, just like Q! designer Thomas Willemeit of GRAFT, Hirsch Bedner Associates, INK's creators, talk of a design philosophy that involves 'a stage for the guest's experience as actor and audience'. Confidently rating itself as the coolest, most stylish and sophisticated establishment in Singapore, INK has a strict membership policy, Guest List Select, after 10pm, so its design has much to live up to. It is not as radical as that of Q! The Bar, but it is a very international and high quality design, featuring careful attention to detail and a strong identity.

Hirsch Bedner went for a rich, velvet luxury but refrained from being too ostentatious. Materials in dark, soft royal blues, deep burgundies, purple and black, are set against the lighter, harder textures of chrome, wood and stone. The INK logo is subtly woven into the fabric of the design – the curtains, the mirrors, the rest-room door handle – and the glassware, ashtrays and ink-splashed designer uniforms are bespoke.

The vibrant Upper Deck has booths and is designed to suit group revelry rather than tête-à-têtes, while the main bar area is open and the place to be for anyone who wishes to preen and strut. For those who are not seeking attention the Soft Space is, perhaps perversely, a VIP area within a VIP club, and the most decadent area in INK. Obscured by velvet drapes, it's an intimate, boudoir-style space filled with luxuriant textures and loungers adorned with cushions. To fulfil its function as a hotel facility, INK provides three types of environment in the course of a day: lounge, bar and club. However, its design is most successful in the heat of the night when the bar is graced by the glitterati it has gone all out to attract.

The Raffles The Plaza/Swisshotel complex features other crisply designed bars, including the colourful, two-storey New Asia Bar on level 72, which features unusual furniture, a surprising slanting floor and outstanding views. The Introbar, off the Stamford's lobby, is a smart, modern bar popular with businesspeople.

Opposite: Raffles The Plaza, Singapore. INK's main bar area is the place to be seen. It has an unusual bar counter with overlapping sections and a distinctive bottle display

Right: Raffles The Plaza, Singapore. Night-time view of the connected sister hotels Raffles The Plaza and Swisshotel The Stamford dominating the Singapore skyline

Bar	INK Club Bar
Hotel	Raffles The Plaza
Address	80 Bras Basah Road, Singapore 189560
Telephone	+65 6431 5315
Opening hours	Lounge 9.30am–5pm; bar 5pm–10pm; club 10pm–3am (Sat 10pm–4am)
Capacity	192
Design style	Sexy velvet meets clean and contemporary
Clientele	Singapore's elite – celebrities, and the great and the good from the fashion, arts and media industries
Speciality drinks/cocktails	Gold INK, Flaming INK and Red INK cocktails along with Seven Devilish Sins
Music	Alternative dance from Parisian DJ Leomeo
Membership details/door policy	Guest List Select membership, or by invitation only, at night

Above: Raffles The Plaza, Singapore. The elegant lobby of the huge, 769-room hotel

Above: Raffles The Plaza, Singapore. Design no longer stops at the bathroom door. The INK Club fulfils the current expectation for unusual bathrooms with Alessi ceramics, gunmetal-blue tiles with a rainbow lustre, inset sinks and starry mirrors

Left: Raffles The Plaza, Singapore. The upper deck area features red leather booths, illuminated blue floors and reflective ceiling panels

Above: **Raffles The Plaza/Swisshotel The Stamford, Singapore.** The hotel complex houses another of Singapore's most popular bars: the New Asia Bar. Suspended above the main bar and dining areas is the exclusive Club 72

Below: **Raffles The Plaza/Swisshotel The Stamford, Singapore.** The more restrained Introbar is designed for businesspeople and hotel guests, but still features unusual elements like the high tables in front of the bar

A60, 60 Thompson

Thomas O'Brien

Location: New York
Completion date: 2001

Standing tall in the heart of SoHo, the 100-room, 12-storey 60 Thompson has become one of New York's major league, hip hotels. Stephen Jacobs, king of the loft apartment, is its architect, and Thomas O'Brien of Aero Studios (who designed Giorgio Armani's pad in the city) designed the interior. Chic and relaxing, the hotel is immediately distinctive because, unusually, shades of an understated 1940s style have been brought into its contemporary look. Part of 60 Thompson's success is found in its amazing attention to detail in everything from Venetian-style plasterwork to monogrammed toilet paper, Frette sheets and Cerruti-designed uniforms. Another, very significant aspect is that its bars and restaurants appeal to the very sharpest of local talent, including the fashion crowd who mill around the hotel's doorstep.

Situated at the top of the hotel is one of the most exclusive bars in New York. Open-air, with 360-degree views of the city, A60 is accessible only to hotel guests and very select members who hold a prized 'key card'. New York weather being what it is, A60 is open only from late spring to the beginning of autumn, which makes access to it even more desirable. Perhaps it is the city's long hard winters that make this and the pool deck at Soho House New York two of the most happening, celebrity-heavy places in the summer months. The view is excellent – 60 Thompson is the tallest building in the immediate area – and includes the Empire State Building. Set on a stone-slab terrace, the furniture is elegant and stylish, especially the solid wooden-frame chairs, sofas and loungers with comfortable cream cushions. Patterned fold-up stools and silver chairs have a less permanent, garden-furniture look. The bar counter is simple, its frontage decorated with linear lengths of wood. As night falls and the lights of the Manhattan skyline become the main attraction a large square, yellow light against the brickwork marks the bar's location.

The hotel has another, incredibly successful bar which is available to mere mortals and open all year round. Thom's Bar, off the lobby, is consciously dedicated to comfort, combining elements of a gentlemen's club with touches of Eastern promise. Large rust, chocolate brown and wine ottomans are accompanied by slightly worn leather armchairs and velvet banquettes. The sheer, floor-to-ceiling drapes, pale green and white marble fireplace and off-white panelled walls add a touch of class. Customers who are unable to gain admittance to A60 can still enjoy the outdoor life, if not the views of New York, on Thom Bar's covered terrace.

60 Thompson also houses two highly successful restaurants. Thom's serves Asian-influenced American food and is integrated into the hotel, while the brand-new, Kittichai Restaurant offers modern Thai food and is more distinctive, with an exotic design by the Rockwell Group.

Opposite: 60 Thompson, New York. The hotel is the tallest building in the immediate vicinity and makes use of its height with A60, a very exclusive, rooftop bar. Hotel guests and key-card holders can sip cocktails on elegant sofas while enjoying the view of the Empire State Building

Below: 60 Thompson, New York. Like much of the hotel's interior, A60 is calmly stylish without being ostentatious

Bar	A60
Hotel	60 Thompson
Address	60 Thompson Street, New York, NY 10012, USA
Telephone	+1 212 219 2000
Opening hours	Daily 5pm–2am, late spring to early autumn only
Number of seats	30–40
Design style	1940s roof deck, but it's all about the views and the company
Clientele	Russell Crowe, Lenny Kravitz stay at the hotel. Celebrities, models and sugar daddies eye the skyline
Speciality drinks/cocktails	60 Champagne with Stoli Razberi, rasperries and Moët. Head down to Thom's Bar for its famous passionfruit margarita
Music	Distant traffic
Membership details/door policy	Hotel guests and exclusive key-card holders only

Left: **60 Thompson, New York.** As night falls a large square, yellow light on the undecorated brick wall directs customers towards A60's bar counter

Left: **60 Thompson, New York.** The hotel's popular public bar, Thom's Bar, features worn leather armchairs and velvet sofas on a dark-stained timber floor

Left: **60 Thompson, New York.** The bar counter in Thom's Bar is to the left of the room, facing high, pale stools. Full-length curtains and white panelled walls emphasise the airiness of the space

Above: **60 Thompson, New York.** Designed by the Rockwell Group, the hotel's new Kittichai Restaurant opened in 2004. Modern Thai food is complemented by a contemporary, Eastern-style interior

Below: **60 Thompson, New York.** The bar in the Kittichai Restaurant is dominated by a beaten-copper sculpture

Millbank Lounge, City Inn Westminster

PROOF Consultancy

Location: London
Completion date: 2003

Millbank stretches along the Thames and is synonymous with government: the Labour Party's headquarters were, until recently, in Millbank Tower, a short walk away from the Houses of Parliament, and the street itself is surrounded by government buildings. The City Inn Westminster, the largest new hotel built in London for 30 years, nestles in the curve of the tower's lower floors. This led City Inn's chief executive, David Orr, to seek extra panache for its Millbank Lounge, that would reflect the building's Westminster location. He wanted it to have an individual identity that would appeal to style aficionados, visitors to nearby Tate Britain and politicians, as well as to the businesspeople who make up the core of the hotel's residents. It was therefore essential for it to work both day and night.

This kind of multifunctionalism can be a recipe for interior-design disaster, but David J Morris of PROOF Consultancy worked with the internal architecture to pull off a space that works from breakfast time through to the early hours of the next morning. He used the supporting columns to divide the Millbank Lounge into three distinct but complementary zones: Chill, Crush and Chat. The centrepiece is the all-red tongue of the Chill area, which licks out from the similar red of the main section of the bar counter and is flanked by the cream and natural colours of the Crush and Chat spaces. Red strip-lighting, the glass-panel frontage on the bar counter (created by painting red ceramic ink on glass) and leather stools, together with low sofas and soft, glowing barasol ceiling panels, create a sexual, free-flowing space that has made the Millbank Lounge the area's destination bar. Millbank Mules and house speciality whisky cocktails, such as the Kiltlifter, ensure its popularity in what is otherwise a relatively barren part of night-time London.

The use of red is subtly derived from the colours typical of Westminster club culture (rather than New Labour's logo), and the few cream leather armchairs that abut the Chat zone are a more direct reference to this. This area consists of comfortable booths along the length of the all-glass facade, and is more suitable than Chill for politicians' discreet conversations. The booths are broad and the partitions glass, so natural light comes into the rest of the space and customers feel connected to the bar area. On the other side of the bar, Crush's small dining booths are reminiscent of the 1950s, and suitable for lunch or evening drinks if anyone doesn't wish to be fully immersed in the decadence of Chill.

The City Inn Westminster has its own 'side street' – an 'art' street that leads customers from Millbank to the lounge entrance and stresses the hotel's proximity to Tate Britain. It is 80 metres (87 yards) long and features immense engravings on slate by Susanna Heron. Perhaps surprisingly, despite its functional name the City Inn chain is committed to contemporary art, and this is borne out in the lobby. Again designed by PROOF, it contains large artworks and incredibly comfortable, Starckesque miniature armchairs. These typify the interior of the City Inn Westminster – it reflects the hotel's location and its diverse market, and delivers both style and practicality.

Opposite: **City Inn Westminster, London.** The red, central Chill zone stretches out from the bar counter, separating the cream and natural tones of the Crush and window-side Chat zones. The soft red lighting, distinct to this section, comes from barasol panels, which are on hinges for easy interfloor maintenance

Bar	Millbank Lounge
Hotel	City Inn Westminster
Address	30 John Islip Street, London SW1P 4DD, UK
Telephone	+44 (0)20 7630 3000
Opening hours	24-hour (residents), 10am–11pm (non-residents)
Capacity	90 seated, 200 overall capacity
Design style	Modern with a twist. A pulsing red heart buffered by cooler cream
Clientele	Hotel guests plus local media workers, arty crowd from Tate Britain and politicians. Famous faces have included the Scissor Sisters
Speciality drinks/cocktails	Millbank Mules. Whisky cocktails complemented by an extensive library of malts
Music	DJs play tempo house and funk every Friday night
Membership details/door policy	None

Below: **City Inn Westminster, London.** The main section
of the 8-metre (26-foot) bar counter is almost entirely red
and very alluring. The front was created by painting ceramic
ink on glass. The original specification for red mirrored glass
was unworkable

Below: City Inn Westminster, London. The red Chill zone forms a tongue that leads down the middle of the Millbank Lounge from the bar counter. The seating is designed to make it a communal, sociable and free-form space

Bottom: City Inn Westminster, London. View from the Millbank Lounge's Crush zone, which features additional standing areas towards the bar counter, which is split into a red main section and a blond whisky bar

Right: **City Inn Westminster, London.** The Chat zone consists of reservable booths along the glass facade of the building. Frosted partitions form part of the lamp stands. The booths provide some privacy but don't prevent natural light reaching the rest of the space

Right: **City Inn Westminster, London.** The seating area in the Crush zone has tables for lunch or snacks. The Millbank Lounge features different grades of the same veneer, which provide a textural link throughout its interior

Above: City Inn Westminster, London. The right-hand section of the bar counter is for the Millbank Lounge's wide range of whiskies. Its colours are similar to those in the Crush zone, which leads towards it

Left: City Inn Westminster, London. The finished Millbank Lounge project, with its three zones, remains close to PROOF Consultancy's original concept drawings

Right: City Inn Westminster, London. Floor plan of the Millbank Lounge

Roppongi Hills Club

Conran & Partners

Location: Tokyo
Completion date: 2003

Minoru Mori is the focal point for undiminished confidence in Japan – he will not accept that the bubble economy has burst and will never recover. His investments in both the cultural and economic infrastructure are extraordinarily grand. He almost single-handedly re-created the Roppongi area of Tokyo as a new cultural and entertainment district, and it is here that he built the new Roppongi Hills Mori Tower, a building that is typical of his determination, grandiosity and philosophy. It is a 54-storey office tower, the top five levels of which are given over to an arts, education and entertainment complex, including the Mori Arts Centre. KPF is its principal architect, with Gluckman Mayner Architects creating the top two floors of the arts complex. For the 51st floor, Mori brought in Terence Conran to design the Roppongi Hills Club, a private members' club that has strong links to the arts centre.

A private members' club may be a very British concept, but the Roppongi Hills Club has a cultural intent that is very Japanese. It has a philosophical linearity that would embarrass its British counterparts, whose members often seem to share the wish to withdraw from society and create an exclusive bubble. In contrast, the Roppongi Hills Club, which is described as a '21st century symposium', is a centre where ideas can be exchanged by those who want to reach beyond its walls to address and improve society. Perhaps this is why one of its major features is a stunning, unbroken 360-degree view of the city. The club is not meant to be a timeless cocoon; it is a vantage point from which to see and understand the world as it rushes past.

This outward-looking intent does not mean that the design of the club is not intimate and comfortable. The feel is very contemporary. The space folds and unfolds through a circular series of visual surprises, with both exterior and interior landscapes altering the viewer's relationship with space. The curtain wall of the exterior is curved, as is the circulation corridor. Careful attention has been paid to the selection of furniture and the creation of different moods in the vast range of facilities, which include bars, restaurants, private dining rooms and conference areas. All the rooms cusp around the central atrium, which reaches up through the top floors of the tower, and are connected by an orbital circulation route. There is a clear orientation to the layout, aided by the structure being made of two ellipses overlaid at right angles to each other, rather than being purely circular.

The heart of the establishment, the large Fifty-One Club room, occupies one end of the narrower ellipse with the Meridiana brasserie at the other end. In between these spaces, the other ellipse is formed on one side by 'play' rooms that consist of informal bars and restaurants including a cocktail bar, a sake bar and a sushi diner. The other side is the 'work' zone, designated for meetings, lunches and entertainment of a business nature, which includes a formal Chinese dining room and a banquet hall. As well as furniture, individually designed colour and lighting schemes play an important part in differentiating the level of formality in each room.

The club is a comfortable, calm and exclusive oasis; but with its emphasis on cultural functions, communication and the exchange of ideas, it has an outward-looking philosophy that is clearly reflected in its design.

Opposite: **Roppongi Hills Club, Tokyo.** The star-filled ceiling of the Star cocktail bar brings the night sky indoors. Classic furniture and a modern colour scheme bring to mind *2001: A Space Odyssey*

Bar	Star Bar
Hotel	Roppongi Hills Club
Address	Roppongi Hills Mori Tower, 6-10-1 Roppongi, Minato-ku, Tokyo 106-6151, Japan
Telephone	+81 (0)3 6406 6001
Opening hours	5pm–11pm
Number of seats	42
Design style	Night view brought inside for lowlit playtime
Clientele	Creative businesspeople who wish to let their hair down
Speciality drinks/cocktails	Monday is Scotch night, while cocktails include Star in the Sky – gin, Parfait Amour, blue curaçao and lemon
Music	Background
Membership details/door policy	Members and their guests only (Y189,000 pa)

Above, left: Roppongi Hills Club, Tokyo. The heart of the club is the large Fifty-One Club room, where members can eat, drink, exchange ideas and have casual meetings while enjoying the view through the floor-to-ceiling glass. Conran & Partners also designed Mori's Ark Hills Club, which houses a large collection of paintings by Le Corbusier

Above, right: Roppongi Hills Club, Tokyo. While much of the design has an international flavour, the Purple Room, within Onjaku, is a modern take on Japanese design. Through the doorway, which is surrounded by modern screens, chair backs can be seen rising from the floor cushions. Onjaku celebrates the Japanese tea-ceremony and is perfect for foreign business guests

Right: Roppongi Hills Club, Tokyo. The reception area of the large Meridiana Italian brasserie. The club is full of curves and sloping walls, while strong colours are used to identify different areas. The Meridiana features an informal bar with a range of healthy drinks, which was specifically designed with women in mind

Opposite, above: Roppongi Hills Club, Tokyo. Looming over the new cultural district of Tokyo, Roppongi Hills Mori Tower is 54 storeys high and provides almost unrivalled views of Tokyo. The new, high-rise area is not without its critics as it can be seen from most parts of the city

Opposite, below: Roppongi Hills Club, Tokyo. Although the sushi bar is one of the club's less formal areas its design is sophisticated. Sushi and a wide range of high-quality sakes are served in this sleek, black and yellow room which features a colourful floral mural

Above: **Roppongi Hills Club, Tokyo.** Guests enjoy a view of Tokyo while the chef prepares their food in the small Amakawa restaurant.

Left: **Roppongi Hills Club, Tokyo.** The Aurora restaurant serves French food and is designed for luxurious pleasure rather than business entertainment. Members can accompany the sommelier into the metal wine-cellar and select their wine

Above: **Roppongi Hills Club, Tokyo.** The 'work' side of the club features the Star Anise, a formal Chinese dining room. It is one of five private rooms where members can impress business colleagues

Right: **Roppongi Hills Club, Tokyo.** The orbital circulation route, with its outward sloping walls, circles the atrium and provides access to the diaspora of rooms

Post Bar, The Fullerton

Hirsch Bedner Associates/Architects 61

Location: Singapore
Completion date: 2000

Prior to their work on the INK Club Bar, the international architects Hirsch Bedner Associates created another hotel bar to service the elite of Singapore. The Post Bar is within The Fullerton, a new hotel in a grand 1928 building whose Doric columns line the Singapore River. Architects 61, who saw to the renovation of the original Raffles hotel, transformed the neo-Palladian building – it shared the style only with Singapore's City Hall and the Supreme Court – which had variously been used as the Chamber of Commerce, the Singapore Club and the General Post Office. This last role gives the bar its name and its main *coup de théâtre*, the post office's original ceiling.

Curiously the Post Bar, which features a Music Room and, for cocktails, the Spirited Bar, is much influenced by New York. It is cosmopolitan and buzzy in the manner of a Big Apple bar, and at lunch time it prides itself on offering a New York-deli-style menu. It could have been tempting to make too much of the high ceiling, but fortunately Hirsch Bedner chose to leave this plain, allowing the intricate, original detailing and panelling to speak for itself in a sublimely grand manner. The décor in the Post Bar, including the chrome-framed, semitransparent frontage of the bar counter, reflects the soft champagne colour of The Fullerton's exterior. This is continued in the rest of the hotel's interior.

Some contemporary, surprising touches give the Post Bar its own distinctive character and mark it out as being a cut above the merely elegant, stylish and comfortable. Both bar areas have polished, inverted cone-shaped tables among neat, solid, light-butterscotch armchairs and cream leather poufs. In the Spirited Bar an organic, crinoline-like lamp sprouts from the floor while a large gauze curtain shrouds the bottle display. In the Music Room, which features New Age and chill-out sounds, a huge mirror in a serrated frame leans at an angle against the wall. The clientele is not without its cool, glamorous element, but it leans towards hotel guests and elite business professionals. If the hotel was in a trendier area than the conservative, financial and civic district, the Post Bar could certainly be a more celebrity-heavy destination.

The lobby level of the hotel includes the Courtyard. Open throughout the day for everything from snacks to cocktails, it has an array of comfortable seating overlooked by trees. Sunlight pouring through the glass ceiling of its angular atrium make it one of the architectural delights of the building. In 2001, The Fullerton received the Urban Redevelopment Authority Architectural Heritage Award for its contribution to the protection of Singapore's built heritage.

Opposite: **The Fullerton, Singapore.** A rare example of neo-Palladian architecture in Singapore, the hotel has a grand presence on the riverside in the city's financial district

Bar	Post Bar
Hotel	The Fullerton
Address	1 Fullerton Square, Singapore 049178
Telephone	+65 6877 8135
Opening hours	Mon–Fri noon–2am, Sat–Sun 5pm–2am
Number of seats	143
Design style	Contemporary furnishings within neo-Palladian grandeur
Clientele	Stylish, wealthy businesspeople and hotel guests with the odd glamorous element
Speciality drinks/cocktails	The fittingly titled Cablegram; lychee martini
Music	New Age and chill-out music
Membership details/door policy	None

Left: The Fullerton, Singapore. The hotel's Grand Staircase is an opulent reflection of the building's important historical status as the former home of the General Post Office, the Chamber of Commerce and the Singapore Club

Left: The Fullerton, Singapore. The Post Bar, one of the most glamorous bars in Singapore, is housed beneath the post office's original ceiling. A sense of traditional style merges with the contemporary touches of a modern boutique hotel

Right: **The Fullerton, Singapore.** The Music Room in the Post Bar is overlooked by the huge mirror in a serrated frame

Right: **The Fullerton, Singapore.** Like the stylish Post Bar, the Courtyard is a fitting place for cocktails. Sunlight streams into the angular, tree-lined atrium which is filled with comfortable sofas and armchairs

Lobby Bar, Hotel Josef

Eva Jiricna

Location: Prague
Completion date: 2002

Hotel Josef, which opened in Prague in 2002, is already laden with awards: an AIA Excellence in Design Award, a Czech Grand Prix Award and the Best Realty Award for Hotel Projects. It also gained extra kudos by being listed as one of *Condé Nast Traveller's* 'Coolest Hotels on the Planet'. Unlike many establishments in this book, the hotel does not include a headline-grabbing bar as an individual entity. It was envisaged the bar would be used only by hotel guests and, consequently, it has been deliberately melded into the overall lobby. The design of Hotel Josef is very pure, and it was perhaps feared that a high-profile bar, with its accompanying celebrity-watching tourists and braying media types, would disturb its consciously created serenity. The hotel already has its fair share of celebrity guests, and the lobby bar is an extension of their privacy bubble – a beautifully designed setting where the game isn't about seeing and being seen.

Hotel Josef was bound to attract a great deal of attention, whatever its intentions. It is the first Czech building that the London-based architect Eva Jiricna has designed since she left Prague in 1968. Her early work includes Prague Castle's Orangery, but she is famous for her interiors for the Joseph fashion stores and other retailers, a Jubilee Line underground station in London and, sadly, her commitment to the unhappy Millennium Dome project. Through her international work she has become notable for her use of glass and white materials, set around unusual, diverting structures. With Hotel Josef, her largest building to date, she has reopened a dialogue with Czech modernism and history while expanding on her signature style. The purpose-built hotel is in the historical Jewish quarter, Josefev, but, perhaps unintentionally, the shadows of the steel-framed sunshades that pattern the entrance facade recall Prague's famous Cubist houses a few miles away. Hotel Josef consists of two blocks connected by a glass corridor that runs along a courtyard. The block to the rear, which includes a large, elegant breakfast room, clearly evokes Czech architecture of the 1930s.

The lobby bar is a majestic, white monochrome, broken only by the pink 'josef' labels on the walls, the black extension of the central, spiral staircase, and the guests themselves. The white bar counter is illuminated, with moulded white stools on the crisp, limestone floor, while the bottle display is a regulated, symmetrical series of panels that recalls the clinicalness of Damien Hirst's Pharmacy. White, straight-backed, high-armed, quasi-modernist chairs decorate the space, which can be viewed through the street-side, floor-to-ceiling glass frontage. Passers-by must envy the clientele in this serene, understated, otherworldly place. The monotone setting draws the eye to the twisting black finial of the glass-stepped, spiral staircase that rises through the floor like the end of a drill – a delightful, sculptural surprise.

Hotel Josef's owners and management may not wish to promote the lobby bar as a destination in its own right, preserving it for its stylish, successful guests, and there may be something of a void between the bar counter and the seating, but it puts many other, wannabe style-bars to shame.

Opposite: Hotel Josef, Prague. The front block of the purpose-built hotel is squeezed between an early 20th-century former police building and a residential block

Below: Hotel Josef, Prague. The steel-framed sunshades give the facade an added quality in the sunlight

Bar	Lobby Bar
Hotel	Hotel Josef
Address	Rybná 20, 110 00 Prague 1, Czech Republic
Telephone	+420 221 700 111
Opening hours	9am–1am
Number of seats	41
Design style	Bleached out contemporary cool
Clientele	Stylish hotel guests and the new Czech cognoscenti with a dash of celebrities
Speciality drinks/cocktails	Champagne
Music	Background
Membership details/door policy	None, but the bar isn't promoted independently of the hotel so it is meant to be a haven for guests

Left: Hotel Josef, Prague. The rear block, including the vast breakfast room, evokes Czech modernist architecture of the 1930s, especially when the white horizontal brise-soleils on the facade are pulled down. The two front blocks are linked by a glass corridor along the edge of the courtyard

Below: Hotel Josef, Prague. The lobby bar is a monochrome delight, with the illuminated white bar counter overlooking the space. The symmetrical bottle display, a few plants and the extension to the spiral staircase provide the only colour

Above: **Hotel Josef, Prague.** The spiral staircase, with steel suspension cables and glass treads, appears to twist up into nothingness

Right: **Hotel Josef, Prague.** The core of the spiral staircase, which leads down to the conference area, rises into the lobby bar to form a twisting sculpture

Below: **Hotel Josef, Prague.** The entire lobby bar area, including the Josef logo, can be seen from the street through full-height glass. The main seating on the limestone floor is white, with a beige banquette against the back wall. The clear glass tables add to the lightness of touch

Hemmesphere,
The Establishment

Justin Hemmes and
Bettina Hemmes

Location: Sydney
Completion date: 2000

The Merivale Group, which has a small chain of outlets, raised its sights with the Establishment, a hotel with a range of bars and restaurants, which opened in 2000. SJB and Hecker Phelan each designed different areas, and Justin and Bettina Hemmes, owners of Merivale, worked with them and were responsible for the overall concept of the hotel and the creative inspiration for its design. The building was formerly George Patterson House, which was severely damaged by fire in 1996, and while some of its original fabric has been reused it has been transformed by the addition of a six-storey tower. As well as 35 rooms and suites, the Establishment includes the Hemmesphere private lounge bar, three public bars, several restaurants, a gaming room and a nightclub.

Hemmesphere, as the name suggests, is the Hemmes' creation of a private world. It is primarily a members' club which, like Bar Seine in New York, draws heavily on Moroccan influences but without the same intimate dimensions. The height of the main room is emphasised by exposed ceiling beams, chandeliers and an unusual iron screen. The windows are arched to suit the North African and Middle Eastern array of seating: low, cushion-laden divans and small ottomans. These are counterbalanced by plush contemporary sofas and leather armchairs that add a clubby element to the space, as does the custom-designed humidor and consequent cigar smoke. Patrons who find the eclectic, exotic feel and multicoloured carpet too much can head for the bar with its clean stone flooring and white marble bar counter, or to sushi-e, a Japanese restaurant within the club. Here, low, white seating pods and high stools surround the rectangular, blue-veined marble serving counter.

One of the other successes of the Establishment is its main public bar. A beautifully grand, traditional hall, it evokes the history of George Patterson House with its high, decorated metal ceiling and white cast-iron pillars. White marble makes its appearance again, this time rather grandly in the form of a 42-metre (138-foot) bar counter that runs almost the entire length of the room. Bulbous, modern chandeliers are suspended above it. The original brick walls are painted white while limestone floors, partially inlaid with mosaic tiles, give the room a sophisticated sheen. The bar leads into the Garden Bar, where a new glass atrium covers damaged columns and rough walls that have been left as a reminder of the 1996 fire.

A further, silk-lined cocktail bar forms part of est., the Establishment's fine-dining restaurant. Structurally this is much like the main bar, but there is more emphasis on plush, warm materials.

The Establishment is a bold, multifunctional endeavour, and it has struck a chord with celebrities and locals as well as tourists.

Above: **The Establishment, Sydney.** Hemmesphere is an exclusive private members' club within the Establishment

Opposite: **The Establishment, Sydney.** The Hemmes family bought the remains of George Patterson House, which was destroyed by fire in 1996, and turned it into one of Sydney's premiere hotels with a range of exclusive facilities

Club	Hemmesphere
Hotel	The Establishment
Address	Level 4, 252 George Street, Sydney 2000, Australia
Telephone	+61 (0)2 9240 3040
Opening hours	Tues–Sat 6pm–late, open for lunch Wed–Fri
Number of seats	80
Design style	Moroccan-inspired lounge bar with touches of traditional club style
Clientele	Local urban crowd, VIPs and celebrities
Speciality drinks/cocktails	Absinthe cocktails such as Northern Lights – Green Fairy absinthe, Zubrowka bison vodka, apple schnapps, apple juice, fresh lime and castor sugar
Music	Funky house, funk, laid-back beats. Own CDs are commercially available
Membership details/door policy	Reservations required/VIP membership (Aus $1500 pa)

Above: **The Establishment, Sydney.** The bar of Hemmesphere, with its clean, unfussy materials, provides a link to the Japanese-style courtyard

Left: **The Establishment, Sydney.** Hemmesphere's main room has a strong Moroccan influence, with cushion-covered divans and ottomans among more traditional, gentlemen's-club chairs

Above: **The Establishment, Sydney.** The main bar of the Establishment is a cavernous white room that features a decorative, pressed-metal ceiling, cast-iron pillars and a 42-metre (138-foot) marble bar counter

Bar Miró, Miróhotel

Antonio Miró

Location: Bilbao
Completion date: 2001

Famously, the fortunes of Bilbao, an industrial city in northern Spain, were transformed by the stunning, silver Guggenheim Museum, designed by Frank O Gehry and opened in 1997. It is now such a cultural tourist destination that cities all over Europe are determined to create their own 'Bilbao-effect', commissioning major architects to design iconic public buildings that will single-handedly improve their fortunes. Many are finding that reinvention is not easy. If they all have an equivalent of the Guggenheim the economic effect is watered down; and people are attracted to a city only if it can offer additional touristic pleasures. Once the architectural event has been absorbed, they need to relax, fuel and imbibe in surroundings that are not overly diminished by the building's grandiosity.

Part of the real success of Bilbao has been its growing ability to meet these subsidiary expectations. Other cultural institutions, such as the Museum of Fine Arts, have quickly learnt to make more of themselves, and fashion-label shopping is a significant factor in attracting visitors. However, it is the hotels – and their bars – that are offering the contemporary design surprises that appeal to the people who are drawn to the Gehry building.

Leading figures in Spanish culture have played frontline roles in the reinvention of the city's tourist infrastructure. Javier Mariscal designed the highly acclaimed Gran Hotel Domine and Antonio Miró, one of Spain's most famous fashion designers, created the Miróhotel. The geographic location of both establishments couldn't be more prominent, with the Miróhotel emerging between the Guggenheim and Museum of Fine Arts buildings. Completed in 2001, the 50-room hotel has a green aluminium facade that juts out slightly on to the street. It is not ostentatious, but its large windows and geometrical grid signal the contemporary classiness of the interior.

Inside, the Minimalist finesse of the lobby's white walls and pale woods is balanced with a black marble floor and antique leather seats. The short reception desk with its pale slatted frontage against vibrant yellow walls introduces the theme of the Bar Miró. Here the bar counter, also set on black marble, shares the design of the desk's frontage, with light emerging between the slats. The white leather bar stools, white pillars and white ceiling break up the yellow of the walls, the bottle display and the long, buttoned-banquette along the left-hand side of the space. The heart of the seating area is natural, with wood floorboards, delicate beige chairs and black three-legged tables. There are exclusively designed pieces throughout the hotel, with leather love seats and square basins in the rooms.

Bar Miró is small and simply designed, but its contemporary stylishness and relaxed atmosphere make it one of the city's primary cocktail destinations for tourists and locals alike. The Miróhotel's owners expressly wish the hotel to be ingrained in the cultural reinvigoration of Bilbao, and it has its own contemporary art collection, with Tessio Barba's *La Habana* having pride of place in the bar. The Guggenheim put Bilbao on the map but the city's hotels, and their bars, are helping it to stay there.

Opposite: Miróhotel, Bilbao. The Miróhotel, featuring interiors by Antonio Miró, one of Spain's leading fashion designers, is within 200 metres (218 yards) of the Guggenheim, the Frank O Gehry building that reinvigorated the city and made it a tourist destination

Right: Miróhotel, Bilbao. The green aluminium grid of the upper facade draws attention to the hotel while allowing a great deal of light into the bedrooms. The entrance is simple and contemporary, with huge windows on each side of the door

Bar	Bar Miró
Hotel	Miróhotel
Address	77 Alameda Mazarredo, 48009 Bilbao, Spain
Telephone	+34 94 661 18 80
Opening hours	Breakfast onwards
Number of seats	30
Design style	Contemporary zest
Clientele	Cocktail-loving artsy crowd of locals and tourists
Speciality drinks/cocktails	Good range of cocktails
Music	Jazz to contemporary ambient. Live music every other Thursday
Membership details/door policy	None

Above: Miróhotel, Bilbao. Black and beige are the main themes in the hotel's colour scheme. The lobby features black marble flooring and a mix of contemporary and antique furniture

Right: Miróhotel, Bilbao. The Bar Miró is small, but it is light and contemporary. Wood floors, beige seats and a long yellow banquette draw the eye towards Tessio Barba's artwork on the far wall

Above: **Miróhotel, Bilbao.** The slatted front of the
bar counter is lit from behind. Yellow walls add a
touch of vibrancy to the relaxed atmosphere

Left: **Miróhotel, Bilbao.** The Bar Miró's theme
starts in the reception area. The hotel is proud of its
photography collection

Fusion, SIDE

Matteo Thun

Location: Hamburg
Completion date: 2001

Designed by Jan Störmer of Alsop & Störmer, the impressive glass and grey-green stone facade of SIDE reaches up 12 storeys and announces that the hotel is one of the most impressive new buildings in Hamburg. The vibrant interior design by Matteo Thun is no less interesting. One of Europe's leading designers, Thun's recent work includes the Vigilius Mountain Resort in Italy. As well as working with Störmer's interior architecture, his Minimalist, colour-block-dominated designs for the hotel go hand in hand with lighting by the American theatre director/designer Robert Wilson, who has consistently shocked and delighted operagoers in equal measure.

The public spaces of SIDE contrive to be both Minimalist and intimate. The atrium of the lobby is a vertigo-inducing, eight-storey shard, with interior walls that appear to collapse towards each other, but it gives way to a series of more personal lounges, all of which feature Wilson's artistic lighting displays. Dominated by white walls, pale materials and straight lines, the Eurasian Fusion restaurant is something of a paean to Minimalism, yet its very sophisticated, adjoining Fusion bar has an earthy warmth.

SIDE is considered to be the most fashionable hotel in Hamburg, and Fusion is certainly one of the city's coolest bars. The grey, stone walls and wooden flooring provide a contrasting backdrop to the line of red leather bar stools that sears through the heart of the bar. They culminate in a cutout window displaying candles: blood and fire give the space a real vitality. The rest of the seating is also red, in the same style as the bar stools, with square, boxy seats and very low back rests. The slim bar counter has a heavy, overhanging wooden top that rests on almost translucent panels, while glasses hang or stand in midair, on a silver rail. The result is a perverse displacement of weight, making a play of the suspension of objects. Coloured lighting on the panels behind the bar counter causes a further distortion of image.

There is always the threat that cool, stylish Minimalism can be to the detriment of pleasure – it's hard to picture Bacchus in a Kenzo suit. However, here clean lines and hard materials are mixed with a touch of decadence that gives this very modern bar an epicurean pulse. Nevertheless, just in case the denizens of Hamburg, and the models and film makers, get too carried away, the red seating is firmly fixed. Thun's regimented vision can never be truly disfigured.

Much of the success of SIDE comes from its playfulness. The hotel is a signature building that doesn't take itself too seriously and wants to provoke the senses in an enjoyable manner. Endless touches, both large and small – from Philippe Starck-designed bathtubs and unusual coffee makers, to the constant play of light on vertical surfaces and the eighth-floor terrace with its 360-degree view of the city – turn a pared-down aesthetic into a sensory playground.

Opposite: **SIDE, Hamburg.** The bar stools lead towards the glow of the candle display, a warm focal point cut into the stark stone

Below: **SIDE, Hamburg.** Completed in 2001, the hotel has become one of Hamburg's iconic modern buildings

Bar	Fusion
Hotel	SIDE
Address	Drehbahn 49, 20354 Hamburg, Germany
Telephone	+49 (0)40 30999 0
Opening hours	Noon–2am
Number of seats	50
Design style	Minimalist with a blood-red core
Clientele	Comfortable blend of models, media and mortals
Speciality drinks/cocktails	90 wines and a wide range of cocktails
Music	Wed–Sat DJs play lounge and chill-out music
Membership details/door policy	None

Above: **SIDE, Hamburg.** The vast atrium of the lobby stretches up for eight storeys. It provides an angular canvas for the lighting installation by theatre and opera director Robert Wilson

Left: **SIDE, Hamburg.** The heavy wooden bar top in the Fusion bar sits on the apparently sheer counter, while glasses stand on or are suspended from a thin, silver rail. The red leather stools strike a straight path through the centre of the bar area

Below: **SIDE, Hamburg.** Elevation of Alsop & Störmer's building

Above: **SIDE, Hamburg.** The Fusion bar is attached to the more fervently Minimalist Fusion restaurant, seen in the distance. Outside images are distorted on the panels behind the bar counter

Left and below: **SIDE, Hamburg.** In the lounge, futuristic, pod-like furniture sits below glowing orange and yellow discs in Matteo Thun's playful vision of a modern hotel

retro cool

Delving into the past to seek endorsement for the present is an old trick that hasn't been ignored by the designers of contemporary hotel and members' bars. It is easy to appeal to the mainstream understanding of a luxurious interior with established signifiers: a Louis XVI-style chair is a sure-fire reassurance of luxury. In hotel-bar terms the golden age of design was the Art Deco period of the 1920s and 1930s. Even if the bars were wild and innovative in their time, the style implies class and service, which are also synonymous with the cocktail. For members' clubs, classic mid-Victorian, dark wooden furniture and leather-covered seating signify restrained grandeur. However, the most successful retro designs involve some level of reappraisal of original elements.

The designers of many of the bars in this book, including those that at first appear to be utterly contemporary, crib from both Art Deco and Victorian sources; but the best do so with integrated, delicate references or comic, dramatic gestures. While kicking against conformity and creating daring designs, they still draw upon the traditions of the very thing they are eclipsing. Oversized, buttoned-leather chesterfields and chrome-and-glass light fittings

Retro Cool

are often found in the same contemporary interior, while Philippe Starck, David Collins and Ilse Crawford all invigorate the present with – sometimes humorous – retro elements. In Babington House in Somerset, Crawford reversed one of the Groucho's principles. While the metropolitan club took its inspiration partly from the English country house, Crawford turned the English country house into a club. Babington House can be seen as a marriage of the ideas that lie behind the Groucho and the Schrager hotels. Here elements of the club's home comforts and Schrager's design surprises are bound together in an eclectic retrospection that also infused its forerunners.

The Rivoli at the Ritz in London is more of a full-on retro creation, but even this seems to carry a gleeful, knowing wink from designer Tessa Kennedy. It is a new design rather than a refurbishment of the hotel's bar of the same name, which closed in the 1970s. The golden age of the cocktail is evoked with layer upon layer of expensive and finely detailed Art Deco-inspired elements, but the Rivoli isn't a museum piece. It is a bar that conforms to its clientele's expectations of luxury, but the design is so unbridled that it looks nothing like its 1930s Art Deco equivalent. It is so lavish that Kennedy seems to be playing a humorous game with expectations of luxury while laughing at the strictures of contemporary design.

Other retro designs are about maintaining the history of a particular space. The Redwood Room at the Clift in San Francisco is a great example of how a space can be reborn for the contemporary age without sacrificing the glories that make it historically interesting. By contrast, Javier Mariscal and Fernando Salas have created a real museum piece with Splash & Crash at the Gran Hotel Domine in Bilbao, filling the bar with the best furniture of the late 1950s and the 1960s. However, as in the best museums, the design creates its own, extraordinary adventure while showcasing the past. Splash & Crash finds an added joy in evoking a previous era's vision of the future. The Genevieve in London and the Hudson Bar in New York also play this 'back to the future' game of using retrospective imaginings of the world to come. In doing so, these very different bars draw enticingly on the known and the unknown.

Right: **Babington House, Somerset.** The country retreat for members of London's Soho House private club. Behind the Georgian facade is an eclectic mix of retro and contemporary interiors

Redwood Room, Clift

Philippe Starck

Location: San Francisco
Completion date: 2001

Updating San Francisco's Clift Hotel was a bold undertaking for the Ian Schrager/Philippe Starck partnership. Built in 1913, it was a grand Italian Renaissance-style building that revelled in its original, period detailing. Inside, it housed a later Art Deco room walled with redwood panels that are believed to have been cut from a single tree. Starck has never been shy of making an older building work to fit his own vision, but he approached the Clift hotel, and especially its new Redwood Room bar, with a heightened historical sensitivity.

His design for the bar allows the original redwood panelling to be the main focus of attention. The structure of the room and its gilded ceiling are largely unaltered, and most of the new furnishings are in the deep reddish-brown hue of the panelling. However, while they create a monochromatic whole, the fixtures and fittings are in a wide range of materials and textures. Starck's design uses velvet and embossed or ostrich-pattern leathers for the seating, and an exceedingly long bench is cast in bronze. The tables are warm mahogany with clear glass tops. Translucency and light were introduced into the solid, heavy reddish-brown – the bar counter is surrounded by illuminated glass etched with an Art Deco design, while the leather-seated bar stools have violet, Plexiglass backs. One of the room's new centrepieces is the large, glass-fronted, yellow-lit bottle display.

Enough of the original room remains to appease the history-loving San Franciscans who had taken it to their hearts. Even with the Starck furnishings, contemporary twists and playfulness, and plasma screens showing video art, the space still has an old-world, traditional feel – the Redwood Room is a successful, and surprisingly warm, union of styles. This suits the contradictions of a city that can be summed up as an ancient cable-car ride to the technofuture.

This balance between old and new also enthuses the Clift's other main drinking area. The design of the Living Room is influenced by the style of a traditional English club, with mahogany wall panels that, unusually, extend across the ceiling. Instead of large, Victorian portraits, the panelling is studded with tiny square photographs of toy animals taken by Jean Baptiste Mondino, whose images decorate the Light Bar at London's St Martin's Lane. Much of the furniture is covered in dark velvets, with a smattering of faux fur, while the similarly muted carpet has a pattern of wavy lines in a variety of browns. The tiny photographs and a large, apparently collapsing standard lamp add a tremor to the aura, but the Living Room is, perhaps, one of the most comfortable, subdued interiors Starck has designed.

Above: **Clift, San Francisco.** A redevelopment of a 1913 building, the exterior of the hotel features large arched windows

Opposite: **Clift, San Francisco.** The redwood panels of the 1933, Art Deco Redwood Room are preserved in the new bar where almost all the furnishings are the same deep, reddish-brown colour

Bar	Redwood Room
Hotel	Clift
Address	495 Geary Street, San Francisco, CA 94102, USA
Telephone	+1 415 775 4700
Opening hours	Mon–Sat 4pm–2am
Number of seats	80
Design style	Art Deco, panelled room with Starck's contemporary twists
Clientele	Hip Europeans, techno money-men and West Coast wannabes
Speciality drinks/cocktails	Key Lime Tartini – vanilla vodka, butterscotch schnapps and lime
Music	DJ Mon, Fri, Sat
Membership details/door policy	None

Left: **Clift, San Francisco.** Taking its inspiration from an old-fashioned gentlemen's club, the Living Room panelling sports tiny, square images of toy animals rather than portraits

Left: **Clift, San Francisco.** A standard lamp genuflects towards the Philippe Starck-designed wavy carpet in the Living Room

Opposite: **Clift, San Francisco.** The lobby of the Clift is a surreal invention that features undersized and oversized furniture and a working, 5.5-metre (18-foot) bronze fireplace created by Gerard Garouste

Rivoli Bar, The Ritz London

Tessa Kennedy

Location: London
Completion date: 2001

The new private owners of the Ritz, who took it over in 1995, restored the interior carefully and expensively, right down to the swathes of gold leaf. It is as if modernism never existed; and in truth, within the walls of this château-inspired hotel, it never has. However, it is surprising to find that the seven-storey building, opened in 1906, is one of the earliest significant steel-framed buildings in London.

The hotel interior is in the style of Louis XVI, with the exception of the new Rivoli Bar. The original Rivoli closed in the 1970s, but while the new bar shares its name, which is taken from the rue de Rivoli address of the Paris Ritz, it doesn't share its design or exact location. Tessa Kennedy has created an opulent late-1920s grotto that defies the modern fashion for design restraint. Evoking the golden age of the cocktail, the opening of the new Rivoli Bar coincided with the growing popularity of hotel bars, and came shortly before a renewal of interest in Art Deco, following the Victoria and Albert Museum's major 2003 exhibition.

The Rivoli is a small but luxurious bastion of excess. The room is panelled with a highly polished camphor-wood veneer while the flooring is bamboo, but it is the ceiling that initially draws the eye. The space is dominated by five oyster-like, gilded domes that cup the sprouting glass ribbons of Lalique-style chandeliers (the original, typical Art Deco half-dome lights were just not ostentatious enough). Genuine Lalique panels of Greek figures, originally intended for an ocean liner, punctuate the wall panels in an interesting reversal of fortune: in 1957 Art Deco glass panels, saved when the Plough public house in Notting Hill was demolished, were used in the initial design for the elegant Oriana cruise ship. Mirrored panels in the style of Jean Dunand depict scenes from nature and help to reflect light into the intimate space, which features an onyx bar counter, mohair sofas and, to cap it all, chairs covered in fake leopard-skin.

The Rivoli is never going to acquire cool status, partly because its requirement that men wear jackets sticks in the craw of the independent-minded, new wave of style-savvy cocktail drinkers. However, its unrestrained evocation of decadence makes its design as unique and brave as that of any contemporary hotel bar. It is perhaps a paradox that suits, and even dinner jackets, dominate the couture of the clientele in this free-spirited place, while elsewhere exuberant, youthful creatives are seeking entertainment within rather more straitjacketed modern interiors.

The Ritz London. The Art Deco-style etched window along Arlington Street

The Ritz London. The Rivoli's ceiling features Lalique-style glass chandeliers set in gilded domes. On the very left, the camphor-wood panelling is inset with genuine Lalique panels in a decadent, Greek theme. Art Deco rugs on the bamboo flooring help to create a warm atmosphere

Bar	Rivoli Bar
Hotel	The Ritz London
Address	150 Piccadilly, London W1J 9BR, UK
Telephone	+44 (0)20 7493 8181
Opening hours	Mon–Sat 11.30am–1am, Sun noon–12.30am (residents); Mon–Sat 11.30am–11pm, Sun noon–10.30pm (non-residents)
Number of seats	45
Design style	Eclectic Art Deco
Clientele	Hotel guests, Mayfair residents, London socialites and corporate businesspeople
Speciality drinks/cocktails	Champagne cocktails including the Rivoli – strawberries, Campari, gin and champagne
Music	Strictly background
Membership details/door policy	Gentlemen are required to wear a jacket. No jeans or sportswear

Above and below: **The Ritz London.** The Ritz hotel runs along Piccadilly and overlooks Green Park

Left: **The Ritz London.** Scenes of deer and birds are depicted on four large mirrors, painted in gold- and silver-leaf in the style of the Parisian designer Jean Dunand. The Rivoli is naturally quite dark and the mirrors help to illuminate its features

Above: The Ritz London. Towards the back of the Rivoli. The original domed ceiling lights were replaced by Lalique-style chandeliers

Below: The Ritz London. Straight-backed palisander-wood chairs and armchairs covered in fake leopard-skin provide contrasting textures

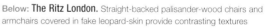

Bungalow 8

Rafael and Diana Viñoly

Location: New York
Completion date: 2001

Bungalow 8 continues to be one of the very hottest, most exclusive places in New York. It's so notoriously difficult to get into it that even well-known actors and celebrities look a little giddy when they gain entry. The exterior of the building ensures the club-lounge's exclusivity: you have to be in the know to even guess what lies beyond it. The Rafael Viñoly-designed, rust-coloured, corrugated-metal facade, in what is a very unprepossessing part of West Chelsea, is totally unmarked, with the exception of a witty 'No Vacancy' sign. Well, witty if you are allowed in – the joke may pall if night-time plans are thwarted at the doorway. The starry-eyed who have got into the club for the first time will be surprised at how small it is. The lounge is essentially a narrow, elongated loft, and would feel even smaller without the steel-framed skylight that opens up the space.

Owner Amy Sacco, whose establishments include the similarly successful Lot 61 in New York, has created a genuinely private, de luxe club, which is inspired by the bungalows of the Beverly Hills Hotel in Los Angeles and owes some debt to the faded glamour of Miami's South Beach. Hiring Rafael Viñoly, whose work includes the Tokyo International Forum and the Kimmel Center for the Performing Arts, was a statement of architectural intent. His partner Diana Viñoly has gone full-out for old school, Hollywood glamour in the interior. With its tall, potted palm trees, Bungalow 8 is like a Los Angeles poolside, but the shimmer of water comes from Lucas Michael's huge photographic murals which run the length of the walls.

Luxury is the order of the day, in both materials and service. Striped and Dalmatian-spotted circular banquettes, and spiky-armed, polka-dot chairs, are the highlights of the furniture, while the flooring is covered with contrasting broad and narrow stripes. Sunlight, regimented by the slats in the skylight, falls across the palm trees to create a tropical atmosphere. There are minibars by the banquettes, and on-site hair stylists just in case anyone fancies a 1940s coiffure to suit the décor.

Hunger pangs can be relieved with a menu that features Tsar Imperial osetra caviar at a mere $1,200 a pop. Finally, if a yellow cab is below anyone's means they can arrange to leave by helicopter. Seriously.

The Viñolys have created a club-lounge that rivals Studio 54 in terms of exclusive notoriety, only with better décor, and that has helped to make Sacco the club queen of New York. Bungalow 8's star is so bright that it must eventually wane, but at least its design has made it worthy of its initial trajectory.

Opposite: Bungalow 8, New York. The exterior of the club-lounge is made of rust-coloured, corrugated metal. The only sign inevitably says 'No vacancy' – there is nothing to suggest what lies behind the facade. The only concession to the public is the overhang to protect some of the waiting crowd from the rain

Below: Bungalow 8, New York. The unmarked building, which sits on a less than enchanting street in West Chelsea, is a night-time hub for the rich and famous. The lounge is converted from a narrow, industrial loft

Club	Bungalow 8
Address	515 West 27th Street, New York, NY 10001-5505, USA
Telephone	+1 212 629 333
Opening hours	10pm–4am
Capacity	100 including standing
Design style	Hollywood glam inspired by the Beverly Hills Hotel bungalows and South Beach-style
Clientele	Older, stylish actors and musicians including Bowie and de Niro, plus the very wealthy
Speciality drinks/cocktails	Champagne
Music	DJ with an eclectic mix including Latin, salsa and lounge
Membership details/door policy	Members only, with a very strict door policy. Look your best and go there on a Monday for easier access

Above: Bungalow 8, New York. Welcome to Beverly Hills. The interior, and the name of the club, is derived from the bungalows of the Beverly Hills Hotel. The tropical, poolside feel is reinforced by the palm trees and light coming through the long, steel-framed skylight

Right: Bungalow 8, New York. Seating includes a series of almost circular spotted and striped banquettes that cup reflective tables

Above: **Bungalow 8, New York.** The lower walls are decorated with Lucas Michael's huge photographic murals, which capture the faded glamour of poolside life

Below: **Bungalow 8, New York.** The rich and famous can relax by the pool in Lucas Michael's photograph and pretend they are back on the West Coast rather than in the heart of New York

Below: **Bungalow 8, New York.** Hollywood glamour doesn't stop at the bathroom dor. Mirrored walls, mosaic surfaces and steel fittings provide Bungalow 8's most nightclub-like area

Babington House

Ilse Crawford

Location: Somerset
Completion date: 1999

The decision by Nick Jones, owner of London's Soho House, to create a country retreat for the celebrity-heavy clientele of his highly fashionable members' club, was a masterstroke. The result, Babington House, is a reinvention of the concepts of the country house hotel and the country club, and it was at the forefront of a trend that now includes Cowley Manor, Whatley Manor and the Grove. Country estates today seem to be awash with red-eyed celebrities and media aficionados trying to restore their sanity away from the flash-popping, urban crush.

Designer Ilse Crawford, who was later to work on Nick Jones's Soho House New York project, took on the brief once Jones had alighted on a Grade II listed Georgian manor house in Somerset. The interior is the forerunner of what was to become Crawford's signature style or, rather, nonstyle: her decisions are delineated only by quality, beauty and comfort. Distressed chic, 1960s furniture, traditional French elegance and contemporary Minimalism all win out in different rooms in this temple to eclecticism.

The free design style suits the relaxed Babington ethic. Guests can eat or drink at any time, virtually wherever they like. The Log Room, with its long, black leather banquettes and end wall consisting of a floor-to-ceiling stack of on-end logs, is the most formal eating area, but visitors may choose to head for the terrace or a buttoned-leather sofa in the Pool Room. The House Bar, on the ground floor, has a curving central bar counter, single-stem, leather-topped bar stools and low-hanging orbs of light. Its open fire, comfortable sofas and large plasma screens ensure that there is a safe, protective haven from the onslaught of the Cowshed. Based around a building named after its former use, this is a health and beauty centre for celebs whose weekend away is for physical revitalisation rather than somnolent whisky-supping.

The Cowshed includes indoor and outdoor graphite pools, and a gym, sauna, steam room and aroma room, along with the wide range of treatments available in the yurt (Mongolian tent). However, there is also a bar for those whose idea of outdoor activity is lying on one of the stylish white recliners alongside the outside pool. Crawford merged the Cowshed concept of Babington with the urbanity of London's Soho House when she designed Soho House New York.

Inside, the Playroom is designed with cocktail drinking in mind. Its grey walls, hanging wicker cradles, 1960s-style seating and a central, white oval table make it a suitably refined, but not ostentatious, room. Here, the media luvvies (who want to get away from it all but doubtless end up chatting to each other) can sip their martinis into the early hours before making their way up to one of the 28 individually designed, comfy-chic rooms.

Members of Soho House are automatically members of Babington, and people living within a 48-kilometre (30-mile) radius of the house can apply for membership and use the facilities, including the Cowshed. Depending on availability, mere mortals are able to book rooms.

Above: **Babington House, Somerset.** The country house hotel is reborn with humorous, contemporary twists that appeal to its media clientele

Opposite: **Babington House, Somerset.** Set in lush countryside, the Georgian Grade II listed manor house is only two hours from bustling London

Hotel	Babington House
Address	Babington, nr Frome, Somerset BA11 3RW, UK
Telephone	+44 (0)1373 812 266
Opening hours	House bar Mon–Sun 8am–3am
Design style	Georgian country house, with eclectic postwar furniture and modern technology
Clientele	Soho House's media stars get out their chunky jumpers. Zoe Ball and Norman Cook got married here. Madonna has a favourite room
Speciality drinks/cocktails	The usual range
Music	Sultry, contemporary
Membership details/door policy	Soho House members (£500 pa), local members (£700 pa, includes Soho House membership) and hotel guests only

Above: **Babington House, Somerset.** The Playroom, a favourite place for late-night cocktails, is more thematically stylised than most of the interior. Hanging wicker cradles offer an alternative to the 1960s sofas

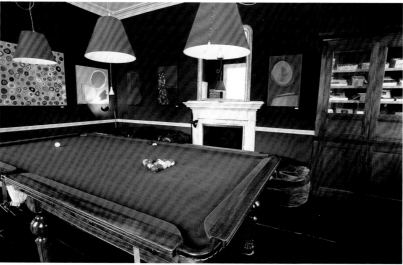

Left: **Babington House, Somerset.** The Pool Room features dark-stained wooden floors, contemporary art and purple baize. As is typical of Ilse Crawford, the furniture throughout the house is eclectic; here it includes a brown, buttoned-leather sofa and a green beanbag

Right: Babington House, Somerset. A bedroom in the main house. Vintage furniture and stylish contemporary oddities like the arcing light are mixed with the latest technology

Below: Babington House, Somerset. The Log Room is the formal restaurant. The long, dark leather banquette adds a touch of sexiness while the far wall is made up of a stack of logs. A glass-fronted fire with a prominent flue warms the room

Above: Babington House, Somerset. Lest guests forget they're in the country, the health and beauty centre is in the Cowshed. Both the indoor pool and the outdoor one further away are heated

Above: Babington House, Somerset. Elegant poolside loungers are lined up against the backdrop of the trees. Guests are free to roam the grounds or recline by the lake

Bar Seine, Hôtel Plaza Athénée

Gettys

Location: New York
Completion date: 2001

Somewhat confusingly, the second to last episode of 'Sex and the City' was shot in Bar Seine at the Hôtel Plaza Athénée in New York, while the last one was filmed in Le Bar of the hotel of the same name in Paris. Both are elegant luxury establishments with highly successful bars, but they are independent of each other and run by different organisations. Whereas Le Bar, redesigned by Patrick Jouin, is a classic, ornate, French interior made contemporary by a huge illuminated, ice-like bar, Bar Seine is a less demonstrative, retrospective step into North Africa.

The New York hotel opened in the 1920s as the Hotel Alrae, and changed its name in 1984. Guests have included Diana, Princess of Wales, and Paul McCartney, and the Hôtel Plaza Athénée has always been known as an elegant place to stay. To match the reputation of its rooms with better public facilities, Gettys of Chicago were given a budget of $1.2 million and commissioned to create the Bar Seine and adjoining Arabelle's Restaurant.

The result is an antidote to the pared-down, light and bright sleekness that tends to dominate new hotel-bar design. Even the lighting is amber, rather than white, in this homage to eclecticism and sensory textures. The leather flooring is sporadically covered with Sultanabad and Agra rugs, and studded with Moroccan olive jars.

Rich, red lacquer and polished Venetian stucco decorate the walls, while velvet curtains grace the doorways. With its vast catalogue of materials including animal-print fabrics, mahogany millwork, onyx sconces, gold leaf and Portoro marble, Bar Seine could be a chaotic, sensory onslaught but the décor is informed by a sense of balance that makes it calm and stylish. It is also very comfortable, with a range of seating from high-backed stools at the discreet bar counter to leather armchairs, sofas and padded, cane chairs.

The lounge area of the bar features circular ottomans covered with leather and velvet. Eclecticism extends to the walls where Moroccan artworks are joined by pieces from Asia, ornate mirrors and a butterfly collection. Bar Seine is an exotic creation, which will never be to everybody's taste, but New York socialites, jet setters and celebrities have welcomed it as a hip alternative to its fast, hard-edged rivals. Part of its appeal seems to lie in its suitability for romantic liaisons – it was recently voted 'Best Spot for Romance' by the New York Post.

Arabelle's Restaurant is totally discreet but as popular as Bar Seine. The classically luxurious, gold-domed room features Louis XIV-style woodwork, embossed-leather chairs and Murano glass chandeliers; its French cuisine is highly rated.

Opposite: Hôtel Plaza Athénée, New York. The recently redesigned new lobby is elegant and traditional, with touches of ostentation that appeal to its international, wealthy clientele

Bar	Bar Seine
Hotel	Hôtel Plaza Athénée
Address	37 East 64th Street, New York, NY 10021, USA
Telephone	+1 212 734 9100
Opening hours	10am–midnight
Number of seats	40
Design style	Plush, North African retro
Clientele	Hotel guests, discerning Manhattanites, business moguls and 'it' girls
Speciality drinks/cocktails	The Crystal Cosmo
Music	Nothing specific
Membership details/door policy	None

Above, right: Hôtel Plaza Athénée, New York.
The Plaza Athénée describes itself as a boutique
hotel, but predates the term. A luxurious, small
hotel, it is regarded as one of the best places to
stay in New York

Above, left: Hôtel Plaza Athénée, New York. The
huge variety of seating in Bar Seine includes leather
and velvet ottomans, and high-backed bar stools

Left: Hôtel Plaza Athénée, New York. Bar Seine,
which featured in the final series of 'Sex and the
City', is peppered with exuberant materials that
include leather flooring and velvet curtains

Opposite: Hôtel Plaza Athénée, New York. The
eclectic, North African-influenced design of Bar
Seine uses lush, warm materials, including red
lacquer walls, to create a warm, cosseted interior

Splash & Crash, Gran Hotel Domine

Javier Mariscal/Fernando Salas

Location: Bilbao
Completion date: 2003

The design of Gran Hotel Domine marks another step in Bilbao's progress to becoming a significant cultural city, which started with the opening of Frank O Gehry's landmark Guggenheim Museum in 1997. The hotel does not shy away from its imposing, titanium neighbour, and instead reflects the building in its mirror-panel facade. The first five-star hotel in the Silken chain, the Gran Hotel Domine cost 19 million euros. It is bold inside as well as out, featuring interiors by Fernando Salas and Javier Mariscal, who are leading lights in Spanish design. The lobby's atrium is home to Mariscal's *Cypress Fossil*, a soaring sculptural tower 26 metres (85 feet) high, made of pebbles held within a skin of wire.

The proximity of the nearby museum has infected the Gran Hotel Domine, which provides an environment for some of the greatest works of 20th-century design. It features three public spaces: Metropol Le Café, the Beltz The Black restaurant and the Splash & Crash lobby bar. All three are very different.

Set within a linear structure the Metropol, which has its own bar, is a direct homage to Bauhaus and 1920s design. The emphasis is on black and white, along with the use of stainless steel, and its large windows look out on the Guggenheim and the museum's huge *Puppy* sculpture by Jeff Koons. The café features objects designed by Gropius, Mies van der Rohe and Le Corbusier. Beltz The Black, a Basque restaurant, is Minimalist in intent, with a great deal of stone and oak, and includes design classics like Dalter's Miranda chairs.

The Splash & Crash cocktail bar is a red-and-white tribute to the 1960s idea of the future, and evokes the new-found spontaneity and freedom that typify the period. The furniture includes classics such as Eero Saarinen's tables and stools, and Ron Arad's Babyboop bowls and Little Albert chairs. These are complemented by newly designed pieces like the white leather sofas by Mariscal and Salas. The silver surround of the bar counter and stainless-steel flooring provide textural surprises while white pillars and walls slope disconcertingly in irregular directions.

Splash & Crash is a funky destination for the art- and design-loving voyeurs who flock to Bilbao. However, only those who choose to stay at the Gran Hotel Domine are able to savour the views of the Guggenheim and the hills beyond it from the open-air Buenavistas Terrace. Another facility that is available only to residents is the Txoko Tranquilo Corner, a library of art and design books, which features a beech-wall tribute to Alvar Aalto and an amazing range of furniture that includes pieces by Charles and Ray Eames, Jacobsen and Castiglioni.

Above: Gran Hotel Domine, Bilbao. The theme of the red-and-white Splash & Crash cocktail bar is the 1960s idea of the future. Furniture includes bar stools by Javier Mariscal and Fernando Salas alongside Eero Saarinen's vintage white-and-red table stools

Bar	Splash & Crash
Hotel	Gran Hotel Domine
Address	C/ Almeda Mazarredo 61, 48009 Bilbao, Spain
Telephone	+34 94 425 33 00
Opening hours	Mon–Thurs, Sun 5pm–1am, Fri–Sat 5pm–2.30am
Number of seats	150
Design style	Red-and-white 1960s vision of the future
Clientele	It's an art- and design-lover's paradise, so expect the most stylish of Guggenheim junkies
Speciality drinks/cocktails	Major league cocktails
Music	Chilled out
Membership details/door policy	None

Above: Gran Hotel Domine, Bilbao. View from the hotel's Buenavistas Terrace overlooking the Guggenheim. The hotel itself is also a type of museum, housing a range of emblematic works of 20th-century design

Left: Gran Hotel Domine, Bilbao. Splash & Crash's interior features Ron Arad's red and white Little Albert chairs and a stainless-steel floor

Opposite: Gran Hotel Domine, Bilbao. Coloured lights add colour to the mostly white interior of Splash & Crash. The room is a maze of irregular, slanting columns

Opposite: **Gran Hotel Domine, Bilbao.** The hotel's wood-clad reception area is next to the entrance to Metropol Le Café

Right: **Gran Hotel Domine, Bilbao.** One of the delights of the Gran Hotel Domine is the Txoko Tranquilo reading corner, where guests can read books on architecture and design while reclining in furniture by some of the 20th-century's foremost designers. The undulating, beech-clad wall is a homage to Alvar Aalto

Below: **Gran Hotel Domine, Bilbao.** The large windows of the black-and-white, Bauhaus-inspired Metropol Le Café look on to Jeff Koons's huge *Puppy* sculpture and the Guggenheim

Genevieve, Lonsdale

Adam and Charles Breeden
with Fusion Architects

Location: London
Completion date: 2003

The location of the award-winning Lonsdale bar has its appeal – it sits between the cool, moneyed and media-laden Ladbroke Grove and Westbourne Grove areas, close to Notting Hill – but the real crowd puller is its interior design, which has had the design-savvy, cocktail cognoscenti humming with pleasure since it opened in January 2003. The Lonsdale's pale-blue, understated facade lies at the end of a quiet residential street. During the day, it's hard to imagine that it conceals such an exuberant, futuristic design or attracts such a peerlessly hip clientele.

Working with Fusion Architects, and with a budget of £2 million, brothers Charles and Adam Breeden created a design born out of a 1970s vision of the future: the Tardis would have looked like this if Doctor Who had had an eye for interiors. The influences in both the main public bar downstairs and the private Genevieve bar upstairs are the same, but outside its own four walls the Lonsdale remains one of a kind. Its outstanding feature is the bubble-cladding on sections of the walls in both bars, which extends to the ceiling in Genevieve. In the public bar downstairs, the bubbles are made of brass but have been treated to give the effect of bronze. Upstairs in Genevieve the design is the same but the material is aluminium, which gives the space a brighter, harder look.

The bubbles make an immediate design statement, marking the Lonsdale out from any other establishment, and it takes some time to realise the level of care that has gone into all aspects of the interior. Above the bar counter in Genevieve, for example, the lights are made up of 80 layers of glass that create a graded purple rainbow effect. In the downstairs public bar a section of the ceiling is dotted with bubble impressions, as if the bubble wall has been hinged down from it. One of the more dominant features of this interior is the atrium-like skylight. Constructed from specialised, fibrous plaster it consists of a telescoping series of rings that increase in brightness as if they are reaching towards a planet's white-hot core.

Returning to earth, the bar counters in both spaces, as well as the stairs in between, are covered in fossilised limestone, which is also used for the flooring of the public bar. All the banquettes are covered with premium hide while the funky, retro 1970s look is further invigorated by a mixture of fun-fur patterns on the low stools. These serve to add a touch of disorganised, sexy fun to the Lonsdale's interior just in case it could be accused of taking itself too seriously. The tables are made from solid teak, sourced from protected forests.

Charles Breeden chose to work with Fusion Architects because of their work on Momo with Mourad Mazouz, who went on to open Sketch. A great fan of the North African restaurant, Breeden also used its audiovisual contractor, Sound Division Group. Music plays an important part in the ambience at the Lonsdale, but he wanted a discreet, as well as powerful, sound system that could be regulated independently over the venue's three floors. Sound Division Group set up the DJ area with an advanced Allen & Heath Xone 62 mixer and installed a large video screen and projector in Genevieve.

The intimate atmosphere in both spaces is helped by the fact that the brothers Breeden continue to have a hands-on approach, and are still regularly seen at the Lonsdsale. They have created a unique, quality interior that readily lends itself to the ongoing cocktail sophistication that has swept London since the mid-1990s. The cocktails have their own designer, Dick Bradsell, who is one of London's greatest mixologists.

Opposite: **Lonsdale, London.** The bubble-cladding in the public bar is brass treated to look like bronze. It gives a dark, amber reflection in contrast to the silver-blue sheen of the bubbles in Genevieve

Bar	Genevieve
Hotel	Lonsdale
Address	48 Lonsdale Road, London W11 3DE, UK
Telephone	+44 (0)20 7727 4080
Opening hours	Mon–Fri 6am–midnight, Sat noon–midnight, Sun noon–11.30pm
Number of seats	60 including standing (plus 240 in the Lonsdale)
Design style	Bubble-covered 1970s vision of the future
Clientele	The height of music, media and film with a few Notting Hill trustafarians thrown in
Speciality drinks/cocktails	The legendary Dick Bradsell's and Henry Besant's creations. Earl Grey Fizz; pear and cinnamon sling includes Luksusowa vodka, fresh pear, crème de mûre, cinnamon sugar and prosecco
Music	DJ playing the latest hip mixes
Membership details/door policy	Members/guest list only. The public bar is downstairs

Right: **Lonsdale, London.** The skylight of the public bar is crafted out of specialised fibrous plaster. It telescopes up in rings of lighter colour, adding a planetary aspect to the sci-fi vision.

Above: **Lonsdale, London.** The low stools in the public bar are covered with 1970s-style, fun-fur patterns and velvets. The tables are solid teak

Right: **Lonsdale, London.** Genevieve, the private bar at the Lonsdale, features aluminium bubble-cladding on the walls and ceiling in homage to a 1970s vision of the future. The bubbles reflect the lighting and offer a warped reflection of the interior

Left: **Lonsdale, London.** Premium materials are used throughout Genevieve, which has a fossilised limestone bar counter and leather banquettes

Hudson Bar, Hudson

Philippe Starck

Location: New York
Completion date: 2000

Following his two London ventures, Ian Schrager returned to New York with the opening of the Hudson, which was converted from the 1938 former clubhouse of the American Women's Association. The city, with its reputation as a melting pot of daring, brashness, creativity and sophistication, has always been his natural environment. It was the setting for his original triumph, the Studio 54 nightclub, and for Morgans, his first foray into the world of hotels back in 1984.

With the Hudson, Schrager and his designer Philippe Starck extended their redefinition of the lifestyle hotel by moving further towards the democratisation of style. Starck's own products, like the Juicy Salif lemon squeezer, are often about bringing art objects into the average home, even if their price sometimes makes this unlikely. A huge 'cheap chic' project, with 1,000 rooms, the Hudson is a work of organised chaos.

Although the Hudson Bar is designed to be more affordable and popular than any other bar in Schrager's hotels it is nevertheless a renegade, ostentatious creation. It does conform in one sense. It blends contemporary design with a retro – in this case 1960s – idea of the future: a successful short cut in the pursuit of cool. However, the conformity stops there. The bar is framed from beneath by a bright white floor made of glass panels, and from above by a fantastical, Blakesian swirl of a ceiling, hand-painted by Francesco Clemente. A tree trunk lies across the floor, and instead of branches it sprouts wooden chair-backs to form a bench. Other pieces of furniture share a yellow theme picked up from the ceiling or a translucency drawn from the floor, but are a diverse mix of Louis XV-style chairs, Plexiglass tables, and vase-shaped or carved African stools.

There are several other drinking areas in the hotel, including the Library where the design reflects the building's history. As in an old clubroom, there is a billiards table, and traditional leather sofas and antique rugs. Books range from film, fashion and art to travel, and there are cyber-desks to cater to the many interests of the typical Schrager customer. Extending the indoor/outdoor theme of the Sanderson in London, the lobby rises to become the Private Park, an interior garden bedecked with ivy, trees and garden furniture. The Hudson also has rooftop gardens, including the Sky Terrace on the 15th floor, where hotel guests can relax on green or slatted-wood loungers and sip cocktails.

Opposite: Hudson, New York. The entrance to the hotel looks tiny in the centre of the building's huge, plain facade. The doorway leads immediately to a glass tunnel that contains an escalator that takes guests up to the lobby

Below: Hudson, New York. The Library has the feel of an old-fashioned clubroom with a 1920s billiards table and classic, leather club-chairs

Bar	Hudson Bar
Hotel	Hudson
Address	356 West 58th Street, New York, NY 10019, USA
Telephone	+1 212 554 6000
Opening hours	Mon–Wed, Sun 4pm–2am, Thurs–Sat 4pm–3am
Number of seats	50
Design style	Spectacular, swirling 1960s-inspired vision of the future
Clientele	Matt Damon, Jennifer Lopez and virtually everyone else has graced this bar at some time. Average clientele is fun and funky
Speciality drinks/cocktails	Polish apple martinis
Music	DJ Thurs–Sat evenings
Membership details/door policy	None

Above: Hudson, New York. The design of the Hudson Bar draws its inspiration from a 1960s view of the near future. Translucent materials are placed in opposition to historical pieces and natural forms, including a tree that sprouts chair backs

Right: Hudson, New York. The Sky Terrace on the 15th floor is for hotel guests who want to enjoy the view of the Hudson River

Above: Hudson, New York. Wall-scaling ivy and 14-metre (45-foot) trees reach up to the glass-covered Private Park and its eclectic garden furniture, where guests can eat or drink

Left: Hudson, New York. The wood-panelled rooms are inspired by ocean travel, and also hint at the building's past as a private members' club

Bar and Club Listings

Australia

ECQ Bar
Quay Grand Suites
East Circular Quay
61 Macquarie Street
Sydney 2000
Tel: +61 (0)2 9256 4000
www.mirvachotels.com.au

Hemmesphere
The Establishment
Level 4
252 George Street
Sydney 2000
Tel: +61 (0)2 9240 3040
www.merivale.com/establishment

MINK
Prince of Wales
2b Acland Street
St Kilda
Melbourne 3182
Tel: +61 (0)3 9536 1199
www.theprince.com.au

Czech Republic

Lobby Bar
Hotel Josef
Rybná 20
110 00 Prague 1
Tel: +420 221 700 111
www.hoteljosef.com

France

Senso
Hôtel de la Trémoille
16 rue de la Trémoille
75008 Paris
Tel: +33 (0)1 56 52 14 14
www.tremoille.com

Germany

Blue Bar
Bleibtreu
Bleibtreustrasse 31
10707 Berlin
Tel: +49 (0)30 884 74 0
www.bleibtreu.com

Fusion
SIDE
Drehbahn 49
20354 Hamburg
Tel: +49 (0)40 309 99 0
www.side-hamburg.de

Q! The Bar
Q!
Knesebeckstrasse 67
10623 Berlin
Tel: +49 (0)30 8100 66 0
www.q-berlin.de

Ireland

Morrison Bar
Morrison
Lower Ormond Quay
Dublin 1
Tel: +353 (0)1 887 2400
www.morrisonhotel.ie

Italy

UNA Lounge
UNA Hotel Vittoria
Via Pisana 59
50143 Florence
Tel: +39 055 22771
www.unahotels.it

Japan

Roppongi Hills Club
Roppongi Hills Mori Tower
6-10-1 Roppongi
Minato-ku
Tokyo 106-6151
Tel: +81 (0)3 6406 6001
www.roppongihillsclub.com

Singapore

INK Club Bar
Raffles The Plaza
80 Bras Basah Road
Singapore189560
Tel: +65 6431 5315
www.inkclubbar.com

Long Bar
Raffles
No 1 Beach Road
Singapore 189673
Tel: +65 6412 1229
www.raffles.com

Post Bar
The Fullerton
1 Fullerton Square
Singapore 049178
Tel: +65 6877 8135
www.fullertonhotel.com

Spain

Bar Miró
Miróhotel
77 Alameda Mazarredo,
48009 Bilbao
Tel: +34 94 661 18 80
www.mirohotelbilbao.com

Splash & Crash
Gran Hotel Domine
C/ Alameda Mazarredo 61
48009 Bilbao
Tel: +34 94 425 33 00
www.granhoteldominebilbao.com

United Kingdom

American Bar
The Savoy
Strand
London WC2R 0EU
Tel: +44 (0)20 7836 4343
www.the-savoy-group.com

Babington House
Babington
nr Frome
Somerset BA11 3RW
Tel: +44 (0)1373 812 266
www.babingtonhouse.co.uk

The Blue Bar
The Berkeley
Wilton Place
Knightsbridge
London SW1X 7RL
Tel: +44 (0)20 7235 6000
www.the-berkeley.co.uk

Claridge's Bar
Claridge's
Davies Street
Mayfair
London WIA 2JQ
Tel: +44 (0)20 7629 8860
www.claridges.co.uk

Commonwealth Club
18 Northumberland Avenue
London WC2N 5BJ
Tel: +44 (0)20 7930 6733
www.rcsint.org/club/

Genevieve
The Lonsdale
48 Lonsdale Road
London W11 2DE
Tel: +44 (0)20 7727 4080
www.genevieveuk.com

The Groucho Club
45 Dean Street
London W1V 5AP
Tel: +44 (0)20 7439 4685
www.thegrouchoclub.com

Light Bar
St Martin's Lane
45 St Martin's Lane
London WC2N 4HX
Tel: +44 (0)20 7300 5500
www.morganshotelgroup.com

Lobby Bar
One Aldwych
1 Aldwych
London WC2B 4RH
Tel: +44 (0)20 7300 1000
www.onealdwych.co.uk

Long Bar
Sanderson
50 Berners Street
London W1T 3NG
Tel: +44 (0)20 7300 1400
www.morganshotelgroup.com

Met Bar
The Metropolitan
Old Park Lane
Mayfair
London W1Y 4LB
Tel: +44 (0)20 7447 5757
www.metropolitan.co.uk

Millbank Lounge
City Inn Westminster
30 John Islip Street
London SW1P 4DD
Tel: +44 (0)20 7630 3000
www.cityinn.com/london

MyBar
MyHotel
11–13 Bayley Street
London WC1B 3HD
Tel: +44 (0)20 7667 6000
www.myhotels.co.uk

Reform Club
104 Pall Mall
London SW1Y 5EW
Tel: +44 (0)20 7930 9374

Rivoli Bar
The Ritz London
150 Piccadilly
London W1J 9BR
Tel: +44 (0)20 7493 8181
www.theritzlondon.com

West Bar
Sketch
9 Conduit Street
London W1S 2XG
Tel: +44 (0)870 777 4488
www.sketch.uk.com

United States of America
A60
60 Thompson
60 Thompson Street
New York
NY 10012
Tel: +1 212 219 2000
www.60thompson.com

Bar Seine
Hôtel Plaza Athénée
37 East 64th Street
New York
NY 10021
Tel: +1 212 734 9100
www.plaza-athenee.com

Bungalow 8
515 West 27th Street
New York
NY 10001-5505
Tel: +1 212 629 3333

Hudson Bar
Hudson
356 West 58th Street
New York
NY 10019
Tel: +1 212 554 6000
www.morganshotelgroup.com

Redwood Room
Clift
495 Geary Street
San Francisco
CA 94102
Tel: +1 415 775 4700
www.morganshotelgroup.com

Skybar
Mondrian
8440 Sunset Boulevard
Los Angeles
CA 90069
Tel: +1 323 650 8999
www.morganshotelgroup.com

Soho House New York
29–35 Ninth Avenue
New York
NY 10014
Tel: +1 212 627 9800
www.sohohouseny.com

Further Reading

Books
Of the vast array of publications on the architecture and design of hotels and bars, I found the following most useful:

Alejandro Bahamon, *New Hotels*, Harper Design International (New York), 2003.

David Collins, *New Hotel – Architecture and Design*, Conran Octopus (London), 2001.

Eleanor Curtis, *Hotel Interior Structures*, Wiley-Academy (Chichester), 2001.

Lorraine Farrelly, *Bar and Restaurant Interior Structures*, Wiley-Academy (Chichester), 2003.

Elsa Rocher, *Bar Decors*, Atrium Group (Barcelona), 2003.

Bethan Ryder, *Bar and Club Design*, Laurence King (London), 2002.

Tina Skinner, *Designs for Restaurants and Bars: Inspiration from Hundreds of International Hotels*, Schiffer Publishing Ltd (Atglen), 2002.

Insightful resources for research into the history of specific buildings included:

Marcus Binney, *The Ritz Hotel, London*, Thames and Hudson (London), 1999.

Ruth Craggs, 'Representations of Empire and Commonwealth: A Study of the Royal Commonwealth Building', unpublished dissertation, University of Nottingham, 2004.

Louis Fagan, *The Reform Club: Its Founders and Architect*, Quaritch (London), 1887.

George Woodbridge, *The Reform Club, 1836–1978: A History from the Club's Records*, Clearwater (London), 1978.

Periodicals
While many architecture and design journals naturally include hotels, bars and clubs in the course of their coverage of new design, these specific issues are particularly helpful:

Architectural Design – Club Culture, guest editor Eleanor Curtis, Wiley-Academy (Chichester), vol 73 no 6, Nov/Dec 2003.

Domus Hotel Extra, editor Deyan Sudjic, Editoriale Domus SpA (Milan), vol 864, Nov 2003.

FX, editor Antonia Ward, ETP (Chelmsford), issue 118, Jan 2004.

Sleeper, editor Matt Turner, Mondiale Publishing (Stockport), issue 1, autumn 2004.

Guides
As a guide to what is currently hip – in terms of social kudos rather than specifically in terms of design – these guides often have their finger more or less on the pulse:

The Black Book List New York 2005: Restaurants, Bars, Clubs, Hotels, Evan Schindler et al. Black Books (New York), 2004. The Black Book series also covers Los Angeles, San Francisco and Miami.

Hip Hotels – City, Herbert Ypma. Thames and Hudson (London), 2001 edition.

Time Out Pubs & Bars Guide 2004/5, Time Out (London), 2004.

A directory of some of the classic, commercially available designs drawn from the interiors of the Bar Style projects. Go to the listed websites for further details of products, showrooms and retail outlets.

design for living

Armchairs and Sofas

Swan chair by Arne Jacobsen
Project: Soho House New York
Available from: Fritz Hansen Showroom, 20–22
Rosebery Avenue, London EC1R 4SX, UK
Tel: +44 (0)20 7837 2030
Fax: +44 (0)20 7837 2040
www.fritzhansen.com

Little Albert chair by Ron Arad
Project: Splash & Crash, Gran Hotel Domine
Available from: Moroso, Via Nazionale 60,
33010 Cavalicco, Udine, Italy
Tel: +39 0432 577111
Fax: +39 0432 570761
www.moroso.it

Chesterfield sofa by George Smith
Project: Soho House New York
Available from: George Smith,
73 Spring Street,
New York, NY 10012, USA
Tel: +1 212 226 4747
Fax: +1 212 226 4868
www.georgesmith.com

Louis Ghost by Philippe Starck,
manufactured by Kartell
Project: Hudson Bar, Hudson
Available from: Panik-design, 20 North Twelfth
Street, Milton Keynes MK9 3BT, UK
Tel: +44 (0)1908 259977
Fax: +44 (0)1908 692566
www.panik-design.com

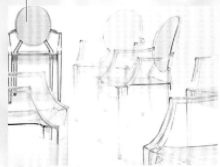

Tulip chair by Eero Saarinen
Project: West Bar, Sketch
Available from: Knoll, 76 Ninth Avenue, 11th
Floor, New York, NY 10011, USA
Tel: +1 212 343 4000
Fax: +1 212 343 4180
www.knollint.com

AND sofa by Fabio Novembre
Project: UNA Hotel Vittoria
Available from: Cappellini,
Via Marconi 35, 22060 Novedrate-CO, Italy
Tel: +39 031 759111
Fax: +39 031 763322
www.cappellini.it

Orange Slice chair F437B by Pierre Paulin
Project: Star Bar, Roppongi Hills Club
Available from: Artifort, Van Leeuwenhoekweg
22, 5480 AC Schijndel, Netherlands
Tel: +31 (0)73 547 70 15
Fax: +31 (0)73 547 70 25
verkoop@artifort.com
www.artifort.com

S32 and S64 cantilever chairs by Mart Stam
Project: Fifty-One Club, Roppongi Hills Club
Available from: Thonet, Michael-Thonet-Strasse1,
Postfach 1520, 35059 Frankenberg/Eder, Germany
Tel: +49 (0)6451 508 0
Fax: +49 (0)6451 508 138
www.thonet.de

Cubica armchair by Paolo Piva
Project: Senso Bar, Hôtel de la Trémoille
Available from: Wittmann Showroom,
Friedrichstrasse 10, A-1010 Vienna, Austria
Tel: +43 1 585 77 25
Fax: +43 1 585 77 25 9
www.wittmann.at

Stools

Morrison stool by O'Driscoll Furniture
Project: Morrison Bar, Morrison
Available from: O'Driscoll Furniture, 26--28
Lombard Street East, Dublin 2, Ireland
Tel: +353 (0)1 671 1069
Fax: +353 (0)1 671 1097
www.oddesign.com

Stool from the Eero Saarinen Collection
Project: Splash & Crash, Gran Hotel Domine
Available from: Knoll, 76 Ninth Avenue,
11th Floor, New York, NY 10011, USA
Tel: +1 212 343 4000
Fax: +1 212 343 4180
www.knollint.com

La Bohème stool/table by
Philippe Starck,
manufactured by Kartell
Project: Hudson Bar, Hudson
Available from: Panik-design, 20
North Twelfth Street, Milton Keynes
MK9 3BT, UK
Tel: +44 (0)1908 259977
Fax: +44 (0)1908 692566
www.panik-design.com

Bar stools from A Rudin
Project: Bar Seine, Hôtel Plaza Athénée
Available from: A Rudin Custom Upholstery, Pacific
Design Center Showroom, 8687 Melrose Avenue
G172, Los Angeles, CA 90069, USA
Tel: +1 310 659 2388
Fax: +1 310 659 1304
www.arudin.com

Flooring

Leather floor with embossed crocodile finish by Alma
Project: The Blue Bar,
The Berkeley
Available from: Alma, 8 Vigo
Street, London W1S 3HJ, UK
Tel: +44 (0)20 7439 0925
Fax: +44 (0)20 7439 0923
www.almahome.co.uk

Mosaic tiles by Bisazza
Project: UNA Lounge,
Una Hotel Vittoria
Available from: Bisazza, Viale
Milano 56, 36041 Alte Vicenza, Italy
Tel: +39 0444 707511
Fax: +39 0444 492088
www.bisazza.com

Leather floor tiles by
Endelman Leather
Project: Bar Seine,
Hôtel Plaza Athénée
Available from: Teddy & Arthur
Edelman Ltd, 979 Third Avenue, 2nd
Floor, New York, NY 10022, USA
Tel: +1 212 751 3339
Fax: +1 212 319 7108
www.edelmanleather.com

Limestone floor
Project: Commonwealth Club
Available from: Mandarin
Showroom, Unit 1, Wonastow
Industrial Estate, Monmouth
NP25 5JB, UK
Tel: +44 (0)1600 715444
Fax: +44 (0)1600 715494
www.mandarinstone.com

Lighting

Romeo soft floor lamp by Philippe Starck, manufactured by Flos
Project: The Groucho Club
Available from: McInnes Cook, 31 Lisson Grove, London NW1 6UB, UK
Tel: +44 (0)20 7258 0600
Fax: +44 (0)20 7723 7005
www.mcinnescook.com

Ming chandelier by Hilliard Lamps
Project: Bar Seine,
Hôtel Plaza Athénée
Available from: Hilliard Lamps, 1433 11th Street, Arcata, California CA 95521, USA
Tel: +1 707 826 1545
Fax: +1 707 826 1561
www/hilliardlamps.com

Max lamp by Max Inc
Project: Soho House New York
Available from: Twentytwentyone, 274 Upper Street, London N1 2UA, UK
Tel: +44 (0)20 7288 1996
www.twentytwentyone.com

Archo by Achille Castiglioni
Project: Babington House
Available from: Twentytwentyone, 274 Upper Street, London N1 2UA, UK
Tel: +44 (0)20 7288 1996
www.twentytwentyone.com

This is a selection of classic cocktails and more modern cocktails with a twist. The measurements are just a guideline as all mixologists have their own take on the perfect balance for even the most traditional cocktails. It is always worthwhile using premium spirits – for instance high-grade Polish/Russian vodka or Bombay Sapphire gin – for optimum flavour.

cocktails

COSMOPOLITAN

Ingredients:

40 ml citrus vodka

25 ml Cointreau

15 ml cranberry juice

10 ml freshly squeezed lime juice

Glass: Cocktail

Method: Shake with ice and strain

Garnish: Orange twist

BLACK ANTOINETTE

Ingredients:

25 ml premium gin such as Bombay Sapphire

25 ml Sambuca

25 ml blackberry purée

Champagne

Glass: Flute

Method: Chill all ingredients. Pour gin, followed by Sambuca, then the blackberry purée into the glass. Gently stir in champagne, filling to top

Garnish: None

MANHATTAN

Ingredients:

50 ml bourbon or rye whisky

25 ml sweet vermouth

2 dashes Angostura bitters

Glass: Cocktail

Method: Stir with ice and strain

Garnish: Orange zest, maraschino cherry

CAIPIRINHA

Ingredients:

50 ml cachaca

2 teaspoons sugar

1 lime, cut into chunks

Glass: Short

Method: Muddle the lime and sugar in the glass, fill with crushed ice, pour over cachaca (distilled, fermented sugarcane) and stir

Garnish: None

VODKA MARTINI

Ingredients:

50 ml premium vodka

10 ml dry vermouth

Glass: Cocktail

Method: Stir with ice and strain. This recipe, with a 5 to 1 ratio, is for a 'wet' martini. The Savoy's original Dry Martini had equal measures of gin and vermouth, but most modern variants of a dry martini involve at least 7 parts gin to 1 part vermouth

Garnish: Lemon zest or olive

BOMBAY FINBAR

Ingredients:

50 ml premium gin

50 ml mango juice

25 ml ginger and lemongrass cordial

Lemonade

Glass: Tall

Method: Shake all the ingredients, except the lemonade, vigorously with ice. Strain into an ice-filled glass and top up with lemonade

Garnish: Lemon slice. Use hollowed length of lemongrass as a straw

MOJITO

Ingredients:

50 ml golden rum

12.5 ml sugar syrup

Juice of 1 lime

6–10 mint leaves

1 dash soda

Glass: Tall

Method: Mix mint, lime and sugar, fill glass with crushed ice, add rum, soda and stir

Garnish: None

SINGAPORE SLING

Ingredients:

50 ml premium gin

20 ml cherry brandy

5 ml grenadine

5 ml Benedictine

1 dash Angostura bitters

1 dash soda water

25 ml fresh orange juice

25 ml fresh lime juice

Glass: Tall

Method: Shake gin, orange, cherry brandy, Benedictine, lime and bitters with ice, strain into glass filled with ice, top with soda, another dash of cherry brandy and grenadine. There are many variants on the Sling. This one is derived from Ngiam Tong Boon's recipe for the Raffles Hotel

Garnish: Lemon slice

BLACK RUSSIAN

Ingredients:
50 ml premium Russian vodka
25 ml coffee liqueur

Glass: Short
Method: Pour vodka into glass containing ice, followed by coffee liqueur. To make a White Russian, add a half-and-half 25 ml shot of milk and cream after the coffee liqueur
Garnish: None

ELEGANT ELLIS

Ingredients:
50 ml premium gin
1 Clementine skin, diced
Juice of half a mandarin
Ginger
Vanilla syrup
1 dash lime juice

Glass: Flute
Method: Infuse the gin by wrapping ginger in gauze, tying it with string and hanging it inside the bottle until the gin reaches the desired strength of flavour. Muddle the diced Clementine skin with vanilla-infused sugar syrup at the bottom of a glass. Fill the glass with crushed ice. Shake the gin, mandarin and lime, strain into the glass and stir
Garnish: Clementine segment

CHAMPAGNE COCKTAIL

Ingredients:
150 ml champagne
25 ml cognac or brandy
1 sugar lump
5 drops Angostura bitters

Glass: Flute
Method: Place the sugar lump in the bottom of the flute. Add the bitters directly onto the sugar. Add cognac or brandy and top with champagne. Classic Champagne Cocktail recipes often exclude the brandy/cognac
Garnish: Lemon or orange zest

OLD FASHIONED

Ingredients:

50 ml bourbon

2 dashes Angostura bitters

5 ml sugar syrup

Glass: Short

Method: Sugar syrup is usually made with 2 parts sugar to 1 part water. Mix the syrup and bitters in the bottom of the glass. Add ice, followed by whisky

Garnish: Lemon or orange twist

MOSCOW MULE

Ingredients:

50 ml premium vodka

25 ml lemon or lime juice

Ginger beer

Glass: Tall

Method: Pour vodka and juice into a tall glass half-filled with ice. Stir and top up with ginger beer

Garnish: Lime

THE SAPPHIRE WOZZY

Ingredients:

50 ml premium gin

50 ml guava juice

15 ml coconut cream

1 dash of lemon juice

Glass: Short

Method: Blend with ice until smooth

Garnish: None